THESE ARE THE
GENERATIONS

THESE ARE THE GENERATIONS

The Story of How One North Korean Family Lived Out the
Great Commission for More Than Fifty Years in the Most
Christian-Hostile Nation in Human History

Mr. and Mrs. Bae, as told to the Rev. Eric Foley

DOERS OF THE WORD

Library of Congress
LCCN: 2012947352

ISBN 978-0-615-67835-1

CONTENTS

FOREWORD:
From the Rev. Eric Foley, Chief Executive Officer, Seoul USA

When my wife and I speak about North Korea at events in the West, people always ask us, "How can we pray for North Korean Christians?" So we asked a group of North Korean underground Christians that question. They answered, "Pray for us? We pray for you!"

When we asked why, they replied, "Because Christians in the West still have some wealth and freedom and power. Most have not yet experienced what it is like when all you have in life is God."

Mr. and Mrs. Bae's story is a testament to the truth that North Korean Christians do not seek pity or yearn primarily for freedom. Instead, constantly in danger of death in the only society in human history ever built as an intentional distortion of Christianity, they seek and yearn for more of God.

It may seem strange to us that North Korea tries so hard to get rid of Christians. After all, North Korea doesn't seem to fear anything else. They have the fourth largest standing army on the planet, with more than 1.1 million soldiers.[i] And they have the largest contingent of special forces in the world[ii] —even more than the United States or China. Economic sanctions don't really slow them down—80 percent of their economy is underground.[iii] They make a billion dollars a year from money laundering and trafficking in illegal drugs.[iv] Weapons sales aren't even calculated in that windfall. So why do they work so hard to kill Christians?

To answer that, we must dismiss the stereotype that North Korea, a Communist country, is also a godless country. The truth is, North Korea is almost certainly the most religious place on earth. And, in fact, the religion of North Korea should look very familiar to Christians.

The religion of North Korea (they prefer the term "ideology") is called Juche, which means "self-reliance."[v] Every week 100 percent of the North Korean population has to gather together, village by village, in special buildings for worshipful services called self-criticism meetings.[vi] Juche even has a trinity—Kim Il Sung, his wife, and his son Kim Jong Il[vii] —and veneration for the latter has not waned in the wake of his death and the ascension to power of his son Kim Jong Un. In the weekly self-criticism meetings, North Koreans sing from a hymnal containing six hundred songs of praise glorifying Kim Il Sung and Kim Jong Il.[viii] North Korea tried to share these hymns with the whole world in 1998 when they attempted to launched a satellite into orbit to broadcast all Juche hymns all the time; sadly for them, it fell back to earth.[ix]

North Koreans pray by looking up reverently at the pictures of the Kim dynasty leaders that have to be hung on the best wall of every home.[x] The original Kim, Kim Il Sung, died in 1994, but North Koreans continue to call him the country's president and regard him as immortal, the god of North Korea.[xi] A Chinese reporter once asked a young North Korean student, "Do you spare a particular time of the day, such as before you go to bed, for Kim [Il Sung]? Do you talk to [him]? Does he talk to you?" "Yes," said the student.[xii]

As for Kim Jong Il, they say a star appeared overhead when Kim Jong Il was born in a humble log cabin in the snowy midwinter. Like one reporter wrote, "All that is missing is the three kings and their camels."[xiii]

If Juche sounds like a twisted imitation of Christianity to you, then you can understand why North Korea works so hard to neutralize it: Only Christianity has the power to unmask Juche as a fraudulent faith. And that is why North Korea has always worked hard to exterminate every Christian within its borders.

Christianity was introduced into North Korea earlier than in South Korea. By 1941, an estimated three hundred thousand North Koreans identified themselves as Christians.[xiv] But the first Christian blood spilled on North Korean soil wasn't under the order of Kim Il Sung. It was under the order of the Japanese, who occupied Korea from 1910 through the end of World War II. Most Korean Christians, under the advice of their pastors, actually did fulfill the requirement to bow at the Japanese Shinto shrines. Not every church complied, however, and those who resisted were persecuted mercilessly. Some fled across the border to northeast China, but the Japanese imperial advance into that area meant the persecution of Korean Christians there as well.

After Korea's liberation from Japan, it was split provisionally into northern and southern administrative zones, with the North under the oversight of the Soviet Union. Christians in this new northern territory resisted Communist influence and, initially, their numbers were strong enough as to constitute a formidable resistance. Kim Il Sung certainly took notice: it would be necessary, he realized, to eradicate Christianity in order to establish Communism.

The government first attacked the church financially, confiscating Christian finances through the 1946 Land Reform Act. In 1949, as the North prepared for war, Kim Il Sung ordered the arrest of everyone who attended religious activities. Christian blood was spilled once again. Untold thousands of believers, their stories lost to history, suffered for Christ.

Following the war, North Korea either demolished church buildings or repurposed them as Kim Il Sung research centers. Christians who did not escape to the South during the war were purged as counterrevolutionaries, publicly executed, or imprisoned in labor and concentration camps. In 1959, anti-Christian literature was propagated by the government. Why Do We Deny Religion? was one such book. It claimed:

For the last three years, the Chosun War and the South Chosun War were triggered in God's name and led by Americans who caused massacre, arson and plunder through inhumane actions. This is proof that religion is the cause of all these things.

Blamed for the war and indicted as coconspirators with the hated Americans, North Korean Christians were executed in increasing numbers throughout the 1960s, and the formal church was completely crushed. The few remaining Christians sought to keep the faith alive through an underground church.

Of necessity, the underground church was not formally organized or networked. Links between believers always proved to be deadly. Pastoral training and oversight was impossible. The majority of Christians worshipped in secret with only family members present. Those who had come to believe in Christ before the end of the Korean War—those who had had comprehensive discipleship training—were aging; the average age of Christians was over sixty. Only a few damaged Bible chapters and crosses remained. Parents could not even talk freely to their own children about God; if they did, the children would be tricked by public schoolteachers into revealing the Christian identity of the family. If a Christian child's parents died before the child turned fifteen, she would never know that her family was Christian.

In the early 1980s, the North Korean government's Korean Christian Foundation opened its first fake church to deceive foreign visitors into thinking that Christians were able to freely practice their religion. In the Foundation's carefully staged services, a small group of state-trained actors used hymns created from the Psalms by the Presbyterian Church of Korea in the mid-1930s. In 1984, the North Korean Communists translated and printed a small number of Bibles and a hymnal. In 1988, they constructed a church building to complete the facade. In 1989, North Korea opened two more fake churches—Bongsu and Chilgol—and staged religious activities, such as Christmas and Easter services, when visitors were present.[xv]

But a new level of genuine religious activity also began during this period—activity that caught the North Koreans by surprise. China became a more open country. In the early 1990s, motivated by South Korean missionaries, ethnic Korean Christians living in China went into North Korea to share the Gospel. Then during the March of Tribulation—the unprecedented period of famine in the mid-1990s—hundreds of thousands of North Koreans escaped to China and Russia, where Christian missionaries led them to faith in Christ. Many became faithful Christians who returned to North Korea with a vision to rebuild the North Korean church.

The number of underground Christians multiplied, as did the number of martyrs. North Korea arrested these new Christians for espionage when they returned to North Korea. First, the Integrity Department investigated individuals based on information from North Korean citizens who betrayed their neighbors out of fear of the government. After being investigated, the Christian was either publicly executed or sent to a concentration camp.

Today, with Kim Jong Un sending out upwards of 40,000 North Korean workers to 40 different countries around the world in an effort to bring desperately needed hard currency into North Korea,[xvi] the likelihood of North Koreans intersecting with the gospel—and bringing it back to North Korea along with the foreign currency—continues to increase. Still, it is impossible for North Korean Christians to admit their faith openly unless they defect and gain citizenship somewhere else, most typically South Korea. There are now more than twenty-three thousand North Korean refugees in South Korea,[xvii] and less than 1 percent of them have personal knowledge of the existence of Christians in North Korea. Most of the refugees came to know God in China, and many are now involved in undertaking or supporting ministry efforts to reach their homeland for the Gospel. Today, the most reliable estimates indicate that there are around one hundred thousand underground Christians inside North Korea.

That's the arc of the North Korean Christian story—the dates, the details, and the statistics. For the last ten years, my wife, Hyun Sook, and I and our brother DH, chief operations officer of Seoul USA, have between us shared that story on every continent. But last year, something happened that amazes me to recount it for you even now. We met a couple—we must call them Mr. and Mrs. Bae in order to safeguard their true identities—whose family has lived out the entire story, from the Japanese persecution through the deepening night of the formation of the North Korean state, through the years of absolute silence and isolation and terror, through the reconnection with missionaries in China, and now through their arrival in South Korea to share their story with the world. Theirs is a family story of miraculous provision and of near starvation; of deliverance from evil and of deliverance into its hands; of belief so bold that it shook villages and of belief so quiet that it passed, undetected yet faithful, under the nose of the ever-watchful state.

It is a story that reveals for the first time to the world just how different the North Korean underground church is from any other church in the world—and thus how surprisingly precious and beautiful and instructive it is. For years, our (incorrect) picture of the North Korean underground church has been that of a more extreme version of the Chinese underground church, with believers toting Bibles and stealing glances over their shoulders as they gather together by the dozens in caves and believers' homes under the cover of night. But the truth of the North Korean church, shown to us over nearly a century in the life of the Bae family in this book, is so fundamentally different from this. As you'll see, North Korean underground Christians are like people who have inherited a small handful of badly bent and faded puzzle pieces. They know that what they have received is inestimably precious, but they have never seen the puzzle-box lid, so they don't know what the picture is that the pieces would make if they had a complete set. They guard the pieces with their lives, and in fact their whole lives are wrapped up in understanding the pieces they have, in ensuring the transmission of these pieces, and in searching for more pieces and for information about the puzzle-box lid.

Almost all the North Korean Christians whose stories you have read are not Christians of this type. They are individuals who recently learned about Christ in China and brought him—and a fair amount of systematic teaching and resources—back with them into North Korea. But the Baes are from an altogether different part of the sheepfold. They are the remnants, born of the martyrs, heirs to the bold faith of their forefathers and foremothers, guardians of the Gospel in the world's darkest corner, God's seven thousand to whom he gave the nearly impossible task of never kneeling to the Baals[xviii] in arguably the most idolatrous country in human history.

"These are the generations," the book of Genesis intones in chapter after chapter. Likewise, these are the generations of the North Korean church. These are the generations of whom we have known next to nothing except the dates, the details, and the statistics that were the footprints that they left. Now they appear before us here in Technicolor—not as larger-than-life saints but as businessmen and bread bakers, prisoners and prophets, evangelists and invisible pillars of an unshakable kingdom.

Mr. and Mrs. Bae are on a mission still, though it is not a personal mission or vision that began with them. It is a trust that they inherited, something they are bound to uphold and bring to completion. What amazes—and humbles—me is the degree to which they have exhibited such costly and complete faithfulness despite having far fewer puzzle pieces than me, not to mention no picture-box lid by which to organize them.

I can still hear the response of North Korean underground Christians to our query several years ago. "You pray for us? We pray for you!" We may have all the puzzle pieces and even the puzzle-box lid, but they, tightly clutching at times only a single-folded, faded puzzle piece inside a trembling, yet reverently closed fist, know and worship and trust the puzzle Maker in ways I have yet to. With my comparative wealth and power and freedom, I am too often wrapped up in far too many puzzles to see that only One truly matters.

June 22, 2012
Seoul, Korea

1. GRANDFATHER:
The Original North Korean Jesus Freak

From Mr. Bae

Some stories of faith are so surprising that you can hardly wait to hear how they end. That's the way I have always felt about my grandfather's stories. As a eleven-year-old boy in North Korea grieving his death, I would beg my grandmother to whisper his stories to me again and again in the dark winter nights, even though we both knew that to retell or even listen to such stories was an act of treason that endangered our whole family. Years later, when I sat on the cold floor of a North Korean prison in one position each day from morning until 10:00 p.m. for more than a year, I'd turn over the smallest detail of one of those stories in my mind for literally days on end. And these days, as I work at the car wash in South Korea in obedience to God's call that I am to raise my daughter as a healer for our broken, divided nation, it is his stories that come to me as my mind drifts heavenward.

I wish you could have known my grandfather. In fact, when I start telling you the story of my grandfather's life—how God would speak to him in a voice so loud that he would nearly go deaf... how, by God's grace, he saved his village time and time again by obeying God's puzzling commands (each more puzzling than the last)... and how he evangelized robbers and invading armies as he sacrificed his body to prevent a church building from being burnt down (while the pastor hid safely out of sight)—I think you will feel tempted to skip to the end of the chapter so you can read how it all turns out.

So I will save you from that temptation by beginning with the end of my grandfather's story:

And so my grandfather burned all the Bibles just as God had commanded him, and thus the North Korean authorities were outsmarted.

And the Gospel continued to spread.

This may sound like a very unusual ending to a story about Christian faithfulness across generations, but North Korea is a very unusual place to be faithful. In North Korea, faithfulness is not something Christians are while they are busy doing other Christian things. It's what they do with their minds and souls and bodies and strength, and it almost always comes at the cost of their lives. So it is a very precious thing, and it means that our stories often have unusual beginnings and unusual endings. Like this one.

My grandfather's story does not begin in North Korea. Of course, in those days there was no North Korea or South Korea—just one Korea, under the brutal domination of a Japanese empire that, in those days, was sweeping across China like a typhoon. But you may be surprised to learn how God commanded my grandfather to stand in the full force of that typhoon and still it in Jesus' name.

But I am getting ahead of myself. Let me start at the beginning.

He will sound like a figure of legend to you. But he was just Grandfather to me—my mother's father and a church elder, though first and foremost God's servant in an evil place and time.

He was equal parts loving and sincere, clever and kind. He was always surrounded by people at all hours of the day, though many just floated near him on the perimeter of a large invisible circle that moved wherever he went. The looks on people's faces as they greeted him—I remember those almost more than I remember his own face. When, as a young man in North Korea, I saw the way those in power treated him, I surged with adolescent pride. He himself was never prideful, though, always stopping to help those in need, always sharing a word of encouragement and his constant admonition to have faith.

My family would look back on those days as a fleeting dream—was there really a time when our family name was revered? To our flesh, they were years of pure gold. But Grandfather would tell us then and much later that God always took care of us, no matter how bleak things seemed.

It was around the time of the Second World War that Grandfather heard God's voice for the first time. He would have had to listen for it above the din of the tanks and mortar fire, as the Japanese advanced steadily through the part of northeast China where my family lived. When my grandmother told me the story of Grandfather and the Japanese, I always wondered where Grandfather learned to speak Japanese so well, in addition to Korean and Chinese. The Japanese army contingent that came to tear down the church that day must have wondered the same thing.

The Japanese oppressed Chinese people in China more than the Korean settlers there. In their minds, the Chinese were uncivilized and dirty, the Koreans slightly less so. But nothing prepared them for the encounter with my grandfather.

He had been fasting for a few days when, according to my grandmother, he heard God summon him—by name—in a voice so loud, so deafeningly loud, that all other sound, even silence, was instantly incinerated.

"Sung do! Sung do! *Sung do!*" the voice thundered. "The Japanese will not harm you. Get close to them."

Get close to the brutalizers who were hunting Christians down and killing them, plowing down their church buildings?

17

When it happened the first time, my grandmother told us, he was sure he had heard wrong. So he just remained there, still, in prayer. The voice repeated the message identically three or four more times.

He concluded his prayers and his fast; concluded that he had indeed heard God's voice; concluded that he had to obey it; concluded that he would stay and develop relationships with the Japanese instead of trying to escape.

Madness. That is what the Japanese battalion must have thought when they came to tear down the church that day. I suspect the church pastor thought that too—from his hiding place. My grandfather, however, calmly blocked the doorway with his own body as he called out to them in Japanese, addressing them as his friends as he asked them please not to tear down the building.

They were stunned to see a human shield, let alone a Japanese-speaking one. "There is a guy who speaks Japanese well among the dirty!" they marveled. And they stopped and stood there, immobilized, axes and sledgehammers in hand, as my grandfather explained pleasantly and in perfect Japanese why the church people gathered, who God was, and why they should repent and receive God's invitation in Christ to be reconciled with him eternally. My grandmother reported that many Japanese soldiers became Christians that day. And the church continued to stand.

Some of the Christians had already run away from the village, but others stayed because of my grandfather. He wasn't the pastor, but they followed him. They called him "Jesus Freak" (yes, this was literally his nickname) even into his old age.

I don't know that my grandfather ever really wanted to hear God's voice, since usually when he did, it was a sign that something very bad was about to happen, and my grandfather would need to comport himself in a way exactly the opposite of what common sense and the actions of sensible men would dictate. Like the time shortly after God used him to save the church. He was humble, but I imagine he must have been at least inwardly gratified that the run-in with the Japanese had turned out so well. So when that ear-splitting voice boomed out his name once again, I wonder if he winced just a little bit.

And when the voice said, "If you don't want the people in your town to die, leave the village and go to work," it certainly left him in an awkward spot. Go to work? He asked God for more details because he wasn't sure what to do. But the more details he received, the less comforted he became. Go and ask every villager, Christian and non, to give him everything they owned, the voice instructed him. Mention nothing about God in the process. Take whatever is given to a faraway place. Invest it. Then return to the village in forty days.

It must have been humbling for him to go door-to-door to make this request. Of course, some villagers scoffed at him and ridiculed him, but you might be surprised how few. After all, even though everyone—Christian and non—called him "Jesus Freak," they could not doubt his courage and skill and favor with God in the face of the Japanese invaders. And I am sure God softened the hearts of many to send my grandfather off with a modest supply of money. There were even some whose crops had failed who entrusted him with everything they had left.

Nearly forty days after my grandfather left town, the Mafia came. They swooped down into the village from the surrounding mountains. They came like locusts and robbed everything and everyone. As my grandmother said (she and the rest of our family were still there, after all), they didn't even leave so much as a baby chick behind.

The villagers couldn't help but notice that the day after the Mafia left town was the day my grandfather was due to return. But he didn't show up.

So the next day, a villager came to my grandmother's house and began haranguing her angrily about the whole situation.

He actually grabbed her and beat her head against the wall repeatedly.

The other villagers weren't much better. They were in the poorest of conditions. Many were starving due to the crop failures that had occurred even before the bandits arrived. So to my grandmother's credit, she went door-to-door and shared her remaining food with each family, encouraging them to be patient for my grandfather's return. Some were touched and said they would wait, even if it meant they would die before he returned. But others still complained.

Finally, after giving away all her food and not eating at all for days, she became weak and lost hope. Forty-three days after Grandfather had left, my grandmother decided she would kill herself if he did not return that day. With this resolution firmly in mind, she led her children down to the dock.

My grandfather always wore a white scarf around his neck. At dawn, while my grandmother and her children were waiting, the sun was rising. A boat was approaching, but she could not make out who was aboard because of the glare. But then she could make out a figure on deck who was wearing something white, and she remembered his scarf. Then she saw the figure waving a white scarf at her. She took off a piece of her clothing and waved back. It was him!

As the ship approached, she and her children started dancing and crying. She wanted to go summon her neighbors, but she couldn't. She was starving and not able to walk more.

He had been gone for forty-three days. Some old and young had also gathered there at the dock that day; my grandfather was their only hope. My grandmother says that they had come to see if there was anything to eat and, if not, they planned to die there too. She said that by the time Grandfather's ship tied up at the dock, the port looked like a white sand beach because of how many people had assembled there.

With such a crowd present and pressing in on them, there was no time for personal greetings or any exchange of information between them. Someone had to address this eager, hungry crowd, and my grandmother, empowered by this blessed and very fortunate turn of events, appointed herself for the task.

She stood on the top of the ship and faced the villagers who had recently been so hostile to her. The first thing she said was that she wouldn't give out any of the food from the ship because they had been so cruel and violent. She chided them for not trusting her and her husband or considering that he might have encountered some unavoidable and entirely understandable delay. She pointed out that the ship was overflowing with food but that the food would not be distributed due to the hard-heartedness of those who had, for example, put her head through a wall. Everyone sobbed quietly and asked for forgiveness. She went on to remind them that she had never deceived the villagers but only sacrificed herself and her own food for them.

Then, my grandfather tapped her gently on the shoulder and said, "Wait. Let me talk to them." He turned to the crowd and began to address them, saying that his was the work of ministry—leading people to God. Not to make money, he assured them, but to promote obedience to God because, after all, God was the One who had asked him to save the village in the first place. He explained to everyone that he was a Christian and he knew that what he was sharing would be hard for non-Christians to understand. So he pointed out to them that if he had not left for business, the money the villagers had given him would have been taken by the robbers. This gave him confidence that it was God who had sent him away to save the villagers, and so the obvious thing for everyone to do would be to believe in God. He told them that God had enabled him to make so much money that the villagers would have enough to eat for the next several years. All the believers and even the nonbelievers nodded approvingly as they listened to him.

Then he asked for those who had trusted him and given money to him to stand on one side. He announced that each of these investors would receive one hundred times more than what they had given him. *One hundred times!*

The others were ashamed of themselves and began to beg my grandparents to save them too. They chanted together, "Save us! Save us! Save us!" My grandfather said he would only trust those who had helped him, but he emphasized that God had surely asked him to leave in order to save the whole village. So he asked the remaining villagers, "Will you now believe in God?" They answered, "Yes! Yes! We believe in God!" They didn't sound like starving people as they waved their hands and cheered at the top of their lungs.

What happened next surprised everyone. Grandfather provided everyone with exactly the same amount of food, whether they had supported him or not. And that is how everyone in the village started going to church.

After all of this, you can imagine that Grandfather was riding an almost unprecedented wave of popularity. So, when once again, very shortly after his return, that deafening voice punctured the silence of his prayer and fasting and called him by name, he must have wanted to hide. And when that voice ordered him to leave the village *immediately* and take his family with him, I can understand why he initially resisted. After all, he had built an impeccable reputation among the villagers. Church protector! Businessman par excellence! Evangelist without peer!

But the voice insisted, saying it was time to save the village one more time—this time by leaving it. My grandfather and family trudged slowly out of town, while puzzled villagers observed in wonderment. *What a strange man*, they thought. *Right after he achieves everything, he leaves it all behind for nothing.*

They probably thought a lot about that strange man and his strange God's pledge to save the village when, shortly after my grandfather's departure, an outbreak of typhoid decimated the village. Many died or were disabled. But our family had been protected, by the grace of God.

But what about the promise that my grandfather would save the village? That may be the strangest story of all. When Grandfather left, he and the family moved to their cousins' village. But that village was in terrible shape—rich neighbors, robbers, thieves, and so many wicked people living there. It was a virtual Sodom and Gomorrah.

They unpacked their bags and started living there. After spending the next year helping the poor, as was their custom, Grandfather and the family found themselves in difficult conditions. Their house was broken into and robbed. My grandmother lamented, but my grandfather kept praying. My grandfather believed they were being tested by God so he could see if they had faith in him or not.

After another year, my grandfather heard from God again. It was the same message: "You will save the villagers." He heard it three times, as loudly as ever.

So he discussed it with his wife. She was worried because they didn't even have food to eat. How could they save themselves, let alone their old village? She figured he must be thinking to leave on business again, and I imagine she probably didn't want her head put through another wall. But he pledged to stay, saying that God didn't tell him to go anywhere or do anything. He said they just needed to believe that God must have a purpose and a plan. So they waited.

In these mountain villages, bands of robbers were pretty common. Some seemed to have a conscience of sorts, stealing only from the wealthy, while others were just angry and took everything from everyone. So into the village descended a band of good robbers, ready to rob the rich in the town. Imagine their surprise when a poor man—my grandfather— interrupted their looting in order to educate them, telling them it was a sin to rob any human being. It wasn't a sermon. He

23

wasn't leading them to God. But they stopped, dumbfounded, long enough to listen.

Then the head of the robbers (probably straining for an explanation for why a poor villager would risk his life to protect rich neighbors who obviously had not extended much help to his family) asked my grandfather if he had been born in that village. My grandfather explained that he had not. He introduced himself to the chief bandit as if he were speaking to a distinguished visitor, and he shared that he was actually from such-and-such village, some distance away.

When the chief bandit heard the name of my grandfather's village, he gave a start of recognition. He explained to my grandfather (and my grandmother, who, as usual, was observing everything with keen interest) that his band had recently robbed the rich in that village, and villagers there had shared with him the story of a man who had once saved the village from starvation in the days before typhoid fever had hit. The bandit asked if my grandfather knew of the man.

At this, my grandmother could no longer contain herself. "It's him! It's him!" she shouted. But this puzzled the chief bandit even more. Why, he asked, would such a man leave wealth and reputation in order to move to a village where he had only poverty and neglect?

My grandfather sensed a golden opportunity to lead the chief bandit to the Lord. He shared how God had sent him away from the village in order to save it. All the bandits smirked at this, since my grandfather, poor as he was, hardly seemed in a position to save much of anything.

But my grandfather continued his witness undaunted. He said he believed that God's Word was his life and that he would save the present villagers too. And although he didn't have anything to give anyone at the moment, God would surely speak to him and tell him what to do.

When he said that, the chief bandit broke into laughter. He jerked a thumb over his shoulder in the direction of a large and heavy rice milling machine that several of his henchmen had been dragging along. "We have robbed all the villages in the area," the chief bandit explained, "and now we must move on. This rice milling machine is too heavy for us to take. God has put you in my path at exactly the right moment. Now you may save all the villages!" And all the bandits laughed, though the chief bandit seemed to mean exactly what he said.

As Grandfather went to inspect the machine, the bandits who had been carrying it told him how it had been a very good thing to have in the early days. They also gave him a horse. And so, my grandfather became rich again instantly— the owner of a rice milling machine and a beautiful and useful animal to go along with it.

But my grandfather was far more interested in the souls of the bandits than in the condition of his own finances. So he turned from the milling machine and urged the chief bandit to repent and believe that God is alive. "Give back what you have stolen," he pleaded.

The chief bandit quickly brushed off these thoughts of God and insisted that his band would need the meat and other items they had stolen for the long journey ahead. But as a parting gift, he agreed to give all the villagers some silk for their troubles. And they parted as friends, as Grandfather so often did with his enemies, and the chief bandit offered his hope that my grandfather would indeed save both the villages with the help of his very strange God.

My grandmother said the chief bandit promised to come back again someday, but he never did. By the grace and providence of God, though, my grandfather did indeed save both villages. My grandparents prospered with that rice milling machine, making money and having all the rice they and the other villagers needed.

But it wasn't long before that voice called, "Sung do! Sung do! *Sung do!*" Then, as before, my grandfather was praying.

God said to him, "It is time for you to leave China. Hurry and go to North Korea any way you can, as soon as possible."

So my grandfather told the family. At that time, my mother's older brother was head of the household, taking care of my grandparents. My grandmother asked the children to come. She said, "I can't force you to leave. But I'm leaving. You choose." So my parents, two of my mother's older brothers, and her younger brother and sister all left with my grandparents. There were only two who didn't come out with them—one of my mother's older brothers and her older sister.

God asked them to leave, so they did. When they got out of the country, the Cultural Revolution erupted violently across China. It lasted for ten years and had as its purpose the removal of all the educated people in China from positions of power. You may know that Mao Zedong, the longtime leader of the Communist Revolution in China, was originally the son of peasant farmers. His fourth wife, Jiang Qing, an actress, noted with concern the popularity of Liu Shaoqi, who had succeeded Mao in his state chairman role when Mao's Great Leap Forward had actually set the country very far backward. Jiang Qing stirred Mao to jealousy, insisting that Liu Shaoqi's university lectures were bringing Liu Shaoqi into high stature and respect among the students, who she insisted were being very spoiled.

Not only was Liu Shaoqi removed, but anyone and everyone who could be branded an intellectual was attacked. My parents were teachers prior to the Cultural Revolution, and one of my uncles was a doctor. Each of my family members would have qualified as intellectuals—each, that is, except for the two who had chosen to stay behind in China. So everyone in my family who would have been killed in China had already left for North Korea, saved by the voice of God that had come to my grandfather. Everyone in the family who could be spared in China somehow stayed. Knowing now the decades of grinding repression our descendants would go on to face in North Korea, I can only guess that God in his mercy moved part of us to North Korea and kept part of us in China, each to the country where, despite the harrowing hardships in both places, we would, by his grace, endure and preserve the message of my grandfather's God.

During the Cultural Revolution, socialism was spreading faster than at any other time in China, the Soviet Union, and North Korea, and that meant grave tribulation for Christians. Korea had been liberated from Japan on August 15, 1945. The Soviets liberated North Korea, and they had extensive discussions about who should be named president of the fledgling state. Finally, Kim Il Sung was chosen, since he had engaged in armed struggle against Japan and was well known in North Korea. He was anointed Great Leader, much to the concern of Christians whose fears would all too suddenly come true.

At that time, religious people were drowned in the sea by the State Security Department, stones tied around their necks. Christians came in for special punishment. North Korea idolized Kim Il Sung and overthrew all the other religions as Kim's grip over the country strengthened.

Because I was born in 1958, I have only the stories of my grandparents to know what happened in those early years of persecution. My grandmother would speak in a hushed and warning voice about how the government searched relentlessly from house to house, burning Bibles and apprehending suspected Christians. She told me how the government had dozens of Christians stand on the edge of a cliff and forced them to answer the question, "Will you be loyal to Comrade Kim Il Sung, or will you believe in God?" If out of fear of death they answered "Kim Il Sung," they were "saved"—but if they answered "God," they were pushed off the cliff and into the churning sea. That started in the 1960s, she told me.

From what I heard from the elder brothers and sisters of the faith who survived the liberation of North Korea, at that

27

time anyone who owned a Bible or even a fortune-telling book was in trouble. Every single book like this was seized and burned in giant wood fires. Kim Il Sung was terrified at the thought of any North Korean serving any god, because any god by definition threatened his right to speak as North Korea's sole divine voice.

Few people know that Kim's maternal grandfather was a pastor or that everyone in his family had faith in God. His father, Kim Hyong Jik, had attended Sungsil College, a Christian school in Pyongyang. Kim Hyong Jik had known God since he was young—and so had Kim Il Sung.

But something changed. Kim Il Sung would go on to confiscate—across every square inch of North Korea—the very book that both of his parents and his grandfather and all his family had revered. He sent investigators to every door to find and burn that book and punish its owner wherever it was found. In North Korea, people began publicly to call all religion "superstition"—even as they cowered in their homes. I am amazed that my family managed. There is only one explanation. That voice.

My grandfather lived for six years after moving with the family to North Korea. I was three when we arrived, eleven when he passed away. In those years, I went to my grandfather's house often. He raised corn, so I especially loved to visit whenever the ears were ripe. I would also go there on Sundays, and he would tell me his stories.

In those last six years of his life in North Korea, Grandfather fasted and prayed much of the time. He clearly had a lot on his mind—likely the future of his family and the preservation of the message that had been entrusted to him. My grandmother said it was in those final years that he often heard God's voice, in the evening.

On one such evening, he ran in hurriedly to his wife. "I heard him!" he whispered urgently. "We're running out of time. Remove the books! We don't have enough time!"

It was four kilometers between my house and my grandparents' house. They sent me off at a mad dash to retrieve my mother's Bible. I returned, breathless, and handed the book to my grandmother. She set it atop the other two Bibles our family owned—my grandfather's grand old Bible, and the one belonging to my uncle.

With a look of pained resolve on her face, my grandmother tore page after page from each of the three Bibles and burned them one at a time all night long, until by morning there was nothing left. My grandfather stood guard at the door.

The next morning, an investigator from the State Security Department came to the house. He claimed to have received information from one of our neighbors that there was a gun hidden inside. Interestingly, however, it was on our bookshelves that he searched for that "gun," finding nothing. He left as briskly as he had come.

I asked Grandfather to tell me that story again and again. My mother was about thirty-one or thirty-two years old at that time, and I was a little boy fascinated by this quiet, gentle man who enjoyed the respect of everyone who knew him. More than anything, I was fascinated by his stories. "What happened that night?" I asked him hundreds of times. And he would imitate that voice.

"Sung do! Sung do! *Sung do!*"

"Yes?" Grandfather answered that night. The voice called out to him three times, he said, and each time he answered, "Yes."

Then God said, "It is no longer the time to believe outwardly but time to believe inwardly. The Bibles you have must be burned. You're running out of time now. Do it quickly!" the voice roared.

It was 1967.

And so my grandfather burned all the Bibles just as God had commanded him, and thus the North Korean authorities were outsmarted.

And the Gospel continued to spread.

2. SON:
The Potato-Stealing Christian Ghost Walking Resolutely Out of Town

From Mr. Bae

My earliest memory comes from when I was five. My grandfather and grandmother were praying, eyes closed and heads bowed, mumbling. It frightened me.

It was not their praying that frightened me but what my grandmother told me when she opened her eyes and saw me observing them carefully. She said quietly but firmly, "Don't tell anybody about this. You mustn't tell. If you tell anyone, bad men will come and take you." I never told anyone, of course. But from then on, I was on pins and needles around strangers.

I first heard the Ten Commandments from the lips of my grandfather. He never called them the Ten Commandments, nor did he mention where they came from or who had given them. They were simply ten pieces of advice I would hear him give over and over again to my mother and father and uncle and other family members as we gathered together at my grandparents' house each Sunday morning before dawn. Don't steal. Don't covet. Don't lie. Honor your mother and father. No matter the problem, one of those ten pieces of advice always seemed to be the solution.

North Koreans worked every Sunday, but we would walk the four kilometers from our second-floor apartment in the city to my grandparents' house on the outskirts of town each week without fail. While my grandmother prepared breakfast for us, my grandfather would turn to each of the adults and talk with them, discussing what was good and what was bad in what they each had done that week and advising them how they should think and act differently in the week to come. Don't steal. Don't covet. Don't lie. Honor your mother and father.

Then my grandmother would bring in the food, and everyone in the family would bow their heads and close their eyes, and Grandfather would mumble something before we ate. You wouldn't even call it speaking aloud. It was barely audible, never much more than a whisper. At other times, we were all expected to do the same thing—me included. Child that I was, inevitably my head would bob up and my eyes would crack open. What was everyone mumbling about? Then I'd feel my mother's hand tilting my head from behind, and down I'd go again.

Children in such circumstances don't ask questions, especially if they sense that adults are afraid that someone is listening and they recall that bad men will come and spirit children away who know too much. But when I was nine or ten, my confusion momentarily wrestled my fear into submission and I asked my mother why I had to do this mumbling. "Heaven is always watching," she said intently, "even if you steal a pencil. So when you do wrong, you confess that to heaven. If you don't, you get punished. And when you receive food to eat, you express your thanks."

And that is how I learned to pray. I truly had very little sense of what it all meant, but what child does? I knew it was important. I knew it was dangerous. And I knew that it bound us together with heaven, somehow.

My grandparents' house wasn't the only place our family met for such times. There was a beautiful beach not far from our house, with an inlet of sand and pine trees. Grandfather used to go fishing there, and my father, mother, and other family members would gather around him for what we called "question and answer time." That was the first time I ever heard God's name spoken: Hananim—the Korean word meaning "the one God." It is the word South Korean Christians always use for God, but it is almost never heard in North Korea. When North Koreans speak superstitiously about nature and divine forces they refer to God as Hanulnim—meaning "Lord of heaven," a more general term for divinity. Even when our family would gather together at Grandfather's house each week, that's the word we'd use—Hanulnim. But by the beach that one day, the word shot out of my grandfather's mouth like an arrow slicing the air clean through. "Hananim!" I wondered if I'd misheard somehow.

Whenever Grandfather was sick, Grandmother would lead the weekly gathering. He died six months before she did; their remarkable lives both ending remarkably quietly during this season of inward belief. Neither of them got sick or became senile or suffered from dementia. Both simply died in their sleep.

"More mysterious than ghosts"—that's what my parents said to each other about my grandparents. That was an understandable description—there were the stories of their past, of course, and my grandfather's walking and talking regularly with God even during that final season of life in North Korea. But my grandparents were more than mysterious. I will always remember them as gentle, polite, and respectable. Even as a child, I was awed by their character.

I was eleven years old when they died. It was shortly after that when bad people came and we became mysterious ghosts ourselves.

North Korea has always prided itself on ethnic and racial purity. As a result, even Korean immigrants to North Korea from places like China—people like my family who had left Korea under the Japanese occupation—have never stood much of a chance inside North Korea. Even before the times of mass starvation, immigrants were publicly referred to as "bad people" and largely excluded from public care and decency. The North Korean government never allotted us much work or land, and they closely monitored our movements. I was always called a "dirty kid" in school. We were treated far worse than those who had lived their whole lives within the country's borders. We lived in daily intimidation—and that's exactly how the government wanted it.

I first felt cold, unadulterated terror when I was a fourth grader in elementary school, shortly after my grandparents had passed away. One night, around one or two in the morning, a woman—a former schoolmate of my mother in China—dropped in unexpectedly for a visit. What was even more peculiar was that when she arrived at our apartment, she was wearing only her underwear. She said that she had been set upon by robbers who had taken everything, including her clothes and money. My mother took pity on her, welcomed her in, fed her a meal, and let her sleep with us for the night.

Hospitality, however, can be a deadly mistake in North Korea if you open your home to someone the state considers an undesirable. The next morning before daylight—around five or six—we were stirred by the sound of dogs barking. That was odd, I noted in my half-wakefulness, since we lived in the city—no farming area, no dogs. Then the rest of my sleep was shattered by a hammering on our door moments before it was kicked in. State Security Department agents poured into our tiny space. The sound of their dogs and heavy shoes and the sight of their guns drawn catapulted me permanently out of what little illusion of security I had foolishly assumed until that point in my young life. I literally get goose bumps thinking about it even now.

Mother and Father leapt up and out into the main room of our two-room apartment, while my siblings and I stumbled awake in the bedroom we all shared. The mysterious woman who was newly our guest sprung up instinctively into the crawl space in the interior wall of the bedroom into which we'd stuff our blankets for storage every morning.

It doesn't take long for a band of storming NIS agents to turn a tiny apartment inside out. They found and apprehended our visitor in seconds. They didn't ask us a single question— just turned to my father long enough to order him to come to the police station later in the morning as they marched out with the woman and their dogs and guns and heavy shoes.

When my father arrived at the station shortly thereafter, they chided him angrily that it is every citizen's duty to enroll every guest with the authorities before permitting entrance to their home. The security of the village and the nation was at stake! They demanded to know why my father had hidden the woman. He hadn't hidden anyone, of course—he had just permitted my mother to help this wanderer to conceal her indecency after being robbed. Without waiting for him to answer, they asked him if the woman had given our family a watch.

In those days, watches were like gold. How many watches had she given us, they pressed, and how much opium? They never paused for him to answer. And what could he have said? He knew nothing about the woman other than that she was an old schoolmate of my mother's, who my mother had run into in the marketplace three months prior—just a chance meeting where the two women realized they knew each other from China. They had exchanged pleasantries and my mother had told her where she lived should her old schoolmate ever find occasion to visit. And visit she did, arriving without warning on our doorstep in the middle of the night in her underwear, hardly in a position to give us an account of what had brought her there, let alone offer us a watch or some opium.

Did she have a citizen registration certificate, and did we? they barked. In order for anyone to host someone from another town or village in North Korea, each party has to submit a visitation request. If the proper paperwork isn't completed ahead of time on both ends, punishment ensues for everyone.

Each day for the next five days, my parents had to return to the State Security Department office to be interrogated with the same questions over and over again, all because of the mysterious woman in her underwear. The agents insisted my parents were lying. We were able to piece together gradually that the woman had been involved in some kind of opium business and illegal watch sales; either would have been a serious crime, and together the combination was disastrous—for her and for us. That's why they sent the State Security Department agents to break down our door: The woman had escaped from prison, ditching her prison clothes and trying to ditch the agents who were in hot pursuit. She led them right to my parents' door. I suspect that even had my parents barred the door and denied her entry into the house, the end would have been the same; we were immigrants, after all—"bad people"—and such people receive few breaks in that land. And that is how ten days later, State Security Department agents came and beat on our door again, this time ordering us to immediately load our belongings into their truck and leave our home forever.

The government expelled us to a remote farming village two hours up an unpaved road into the mountains. Regrettably, none of us had ever farmed even a flat piece of land before. We had been landowners in China, after all, and city dwellers always. This village might as well have been on the side of a cliff. Even expert agronomists would have been flummoxed trying to eke out a living in that barrenness.

There were other families there who had also been banished—maybe 5 percent of the population of that sparse settlement, few enough to ensure that the isolation and discrimination we had faced previously would now be intensified. There was a job president, a group leader, and a management director. They treated my parents worse than poorly: we were not just offenders, but immigrant offenders—the lowest social class of all. For each field, there were about fifty people from five families assigned to work it. It was the most foreboding kind of labor imaginable.

It was there, frustrated from insufficient food, that I saw my parents fight for the first time. You can imagine the conversation. My father, exasperated: "Why did you have to help this woman you didn't know anything about? Didn't you suspect anything when she showed up in her underwear?" My mother, resolute: "This was a poor person in need of my help. How can you not help a person in need?" *When I was hungry, you gave me something to eat… When I was naked, you clothed me.* It was a belief that had cost my mother—and every member of our family—everything. Starvation gnawed away at us from the moment of our arrival. It certainly didn't help calm our tempers or heal our aches.

And oh, the aches! From the first day our truck dumped us out in that forlorn outpost, I was pressed into service to help the village. Labor was desperately needed, even if it arrived in the form of a scrawny, untrained boy. I was required to do farmwork and housework and village work and pretty much any kind of work that the leaders imagined a child my age ought to be able to do. I tried my best to be good—and quiet—remembering always that bad people might take me away if I intimated the smallest detail about our unusual family.

But no one asked me anything—they just ordered me gruffly from one job to the next, hour after stifling hour, day after stifling day. It didn't take them very many days or hours to learn that I just wasn't very skilled. And it didn't take me long to learn why everyone, including the youngest children, ambled about the village stoop-shouldered and grimacing all the time: within a few days, I looked exactly the same way. Pain seared through my back twenty-four hours a day, spreading all over my body and out my bloody, callused fingers and toes. Despite my best efforts, the other workers took constant note of how little help I was.

I turned twelve in that village. My birthday was spent cutting firewood and carrying it back to the village via a narrow lip of rock worn precariously smooth on a cliff face high above the jagged, unforgiving ground. It was that narrowness that made the task especially suitable for what the leaders must have regarded as a very expendable twelve-year-old boy. I caught rumors of how at some point in the recent past, a person or a cow, or maybe both, had tumbled to their death due to a misplaced step off that lip. Now, I was daily tasked with navigating that treachery with a load of firewood on my back. I almost killed myself every day.

I grew up almost instantly. I asked my parents why we had to suffer like slaves. My mother said, "We can become human beings after going through all these things. We're being tested now, but we should still live our lives in faith. God will ease the suffering." Her words touched my heart. How could she—or I—know that God was graciously preparing us for what we would each face years later for the far graver crime of bearing his name?

My mother never gave up discipling us, even then. It was there, through her whispers in that windy, frigid, rugged mountain village, that I learned that Grandfather's ten pieces of advice were really the Ten Commandments, given by Hananim, the one God. She would wake us up at night to learn the commandments and pray with her.

It was all very limited, though. We couldn't pray before meals any longer, of course. When I asked why—with that brand of foolishness particular to twelve-year-olds—she explained in her patient whisper that our faithfulness needed to be even more inward than it had been previously due to the greater scrutiny we were now under from the authorities.

We had been exiled to the mountains in late summer. When we arrived, the co-op leadership had provisioned us with meager amounts of rice to last until the harvest. Always their formula was to calculate how much they thought you would need to survive, and then give you half of that. That was the discipline, the punishment to remind offenders that they were not worthy to live and thus should barely survive.

At the harvest, all the families give everything they've raised to the government. Then the government measures how many days everyone has worked and gives them shares accordingly. We had been there four months, and our half share allotments virtually guaranteed that we wouldn't make it through the winter. Despite my mother's careful stewardship, we ran out alarmingly quickly. As we careened toward starvation, we had no choice but to go door-to-door pleading for assistance from our nonoffender neighbors. We received only disgust. Not one of them offered the slightest help. We were immigrant offenders, after all.

So one night, I awoke to my mother massaging my back in sadness. She asked me somberly to go steal some potatoes.

I was stunned. "Mother," I protested, "you taught us not to steal. Now you're asking me to break the commandment. Why?"

She looked at me thoughtfully and whispered, "Because it's a bigger sin to commit suicide."

Be slow to condemn me, then, when I tell you that I would go to the potato field before dawn on many days, when the wind was at its worst and the field at its most forlorn. Most North Koreans didn't start suffering from hunger until the 1990s. Our family nearly starved to death in 1970.

I learned to cut and carry firewood with nothing but small bits of stolen potato in my stomach. This is how God developed my willpower and dogged spirit.

We undoubtedly would have died had God not gifted my father with a keen intellect. Like my grandfather, he spoke Chinese, Japanese, and North Korean. With willpower and a dogged spirit of his own, he resolved to get us out of the situation we were in. So somehow, amid the endless daily farming responsibilities, my father began to study on his own. He borrowed books from the library on how electric transformers worked, how motors operated, how water pumps functioned.

At the farm, the smallest region where my family was assigned was called "Li" and the next smallest unit, twelve kilometers away, was called "Kun." Whenever the date ended in a one, we were granted the day off to travel to the market at the Kun, the only place where supplies were available. With no money and no transportation, the first, eleventh, and twenty-first of every month might have served as nothing more than recurring reminders of our hopelessness. But one market day, after my father had read all the books he could borrow, he set off to walk the twelve kilometers to the Kun. He had everything planned out in his mind. He knew this was our only chance.

At the Kun, he presented himself to someone on the board of farm management. He announced that he knew how to fix electric motors and water pumps, which were always the biggest headaches for the Kun. Mechanics were exceedingly rare in those days, and—since they almost never ended up at places as remote as the Kun—when they did show up, they were treated with great care and affection.

The board was desperate enough to take a chance, so they asked my father to fix a broken motor. He did, by the sheer grace of God. They couldn't believe there was a person in the Li that had this amazing talent. Such a man should come up to the Kun! And that is how we moved from Li to Kun, around the time I entered middle school. That was miraculous, since to move in North Korea always means getting approval from every level of government—no mean feat for immigrant offenders.

The district management office oversaw all the work related to farm machinery, so they assigned my father there as a mechanic. As you can imagine, he was more than a little nervous at first, having only had books as a teacher. But after fixing a few big problems, he became the top mechanic in the district. He was very, very smart.

As the opportunities began to pile up and our pantry began to refill, he did something even more remarkable than repair an engine. You would think a man so recently delivered from the valley of the shadow of death might be equally well delivered from the temptation to practice my family's forbidden faith, let alone share it with others. Yet when his friends visited our home on holidays, my father told them about God.

As far as the state (who of course didn't know anything about his evangelism activities) was concerned, my father was being graciously reformed and raised up despite his unforgivable failings. But as I grew older and more mature, I couldn't believe that he was forced to continue to labor at such a low level. In China, he had been the assistant dean of a university! How could he not be promoted? He was obviously hundreds of times smarter and more cultured than his superiors, and mechanics were regarded as the lowest nonoffender class at that time.

When I was around fifteen or sixteen, I asked my father why he wasn't an executive or a teacher. He replied, "Because I'm not able to become a Communist. No matter how hard you work, if you're not a Communist, you're considered useless. We came from China, and for those from Japan or China, it's almost impossible to get the opportunity to join the Communist Party. Even those who ran universities there will at best spend their lives as farmers and mechanics here. Especially those of us with family members still in China are always suspected of being spies." But he tried to encourage me by saying that maybe my generation would have a better chance of becoming executives.

For every North Korean man, however, the path to executive life—really, the path to anywhere but jail or the grave—passes through the Korean People's Army. Most of us had no choice but to go into the KPA after graduating from our required years of grade school when we turned seventeen or eighteen. Then, once we are discharged from the military, we'd come home to find our certificate of graduation. Most men serve for ten years. I served for ten years and five months due to some very unusual circumstances. And that is how I became a Communist.

No one gets paid in the military. But after ten years of service, you might—just might, with hard work, good connections, and a little bit of intervention—be invited to join the Communist Party. At the time I served, soldiers were treated quite well. I served from the mid-1970s through the mid-1980s. Given the hardships I had experienced previously in my life, my time in the military was comparatively enjoyable. Even after my father got us off the farm, there were still six of us kids to feed. And even though I was the second child, I was treated like the oldest because my older brother wasn't that smart. He had to join the military too. But my family's hopes were really riding on me.

Once in the army, I looked for any opportunity to excel, do a little more, and earn a little notice. Other soldiers watched sports for fun in the fleeting moments of spare time we were given, but recalling my father's example, I used any second of free time to study on my own in order to get ahead. Even though I had always been one of the smallest kids in my school, I stood out for my athletic ability. So when I became a soldier, I practiced volleyball late at night. I knew that as a volleyball player, I could be promoted from platoon to company, company to battalion, and battalion to regiment—like moving from Li to Kun. Mirroring my father's dedication, I went on to win several silver and gold medals in sports competitions. In addition to volleyball, I ran the 100-meter sprint and wrestled in the 68-kilogram division. I was even a champion high jumper.

When I was nineteen, during my second year in the military, I saw an advertisement recruiting people to learn to play the accordion using instruments provided by the Great

Leader Kim Il Sung himself. During the audition I think I impressed everyone with my intellect and my passion to learn, but that positive impression undoubtedly evaporated when I tried confidently to play the instrument while holding it upside down. But after three months, recognized as the quickest learner among fifty trainees, I was pressed into service teaching others. By the time I completed my military service, I had trained approximately three hundred people how to play the accordion.

At that time, soldiers who played music and those who competed in athletics were considered special. Since I could do both, that opened doors for extra recognition—like when members of the military units would compete against one another for honor. The political member over me was in the Communist community, and the regimental commander over me was in the administrative community. One liked my athletic ability, and the other liked my music. Every year on Kim Il Sung's birthday, there would be competitions around singing various songs of loyalty. A typical song would go like this:

> When you leave to join the army, you have no medals/
> honor/decoration.
> But when you return, you become a hero; you'll be
> embraced into someone's bosom!
> My mother took me to the army depot from the hometown
> where I was born, grew up, and had friends.
> I gave my whole body for the Great Leader and the
> Communist Central Committee!

Win a song contest and you'd get noticed, for sure. Win that kind of a contest and score a medal for physical exercise? You'd be a legend.

But given my family background, I needed to be more than a legend in order to become a party member. So not only did I

43

do well on the song contests and excel in the physical exercise competitions, but I also once organized a health propaganda squad promoting how bad smoking and drinking was. And for good measure, I led political activities as well.

Both the regimental commander and the political member regularly marveled at me. But the bottom line was this: For those who served in the military, if their parents were Communists, they would be invited to become Communists too. But, for non-party-member children of deported immigrant families, it would have been easier to score a ticket to the moon. I contented myself by thinking that if I couldn't join the party after my ten years of required service, I might still at least be able to live a decent life like my father. It would be better than stealing potatoes.

One time I got up enough courage to visit the administrator who liked my music. Being an ordinary soldier, I couldn't just drop in on a superior like that and strike up a conversation about my personal life. It wasn't easy to even get a meeting with someone at that level for any reason because the class difference between us was vast. But I had a relationship with him through some missions I had accomplished. So, miraculously, one day I found myself sitting across from this man and blurting out, "Am I doing everything right?"

The commissar snorted. "How am I supposed to know?" he said incredulously. "I would have to check whether you did well or not on your missions in order to know." It would have been entirely proper for him to have dropped the matter right then, but he was kind enough to look into my file. And when he did, he told me that there had never been anyone who had accomplished their missions better than I had. So I seized the moment to press my luck beyond the limits of my uniform and family standing. "Those who entered the military like I did have to be discharged," I noted with as much innocence as I could muster. "I'm twenty-eight years old now and will soon be sent home. When I'm discharged from the military, there won't be anyone else who plays the accordion. Don't you think we should train someone to take my place?"

That made him worry. So he asked me, "Well, why don't you choose someone?"

"Hmm…" I said thoughtfully. "We would have to train such a person for six to twelve months. But I'm not qualified to be a Communist." It was as close to a quid pro quo as anyone could come without being court-martialed on the spot.

He marveled, "I thought you were a Communist! You're not yet, so let's find a way, then."

So every day I completed my work around 10:00 p.m. and then collapsed in bed. But then I would spring up just fifteen minutes later to do the "voluntary loyal time" training. I helped build a house for one hour a night. There were many military leaders there observing me and the others with whom I was competing for attention. They were there to volunteer their loyal time too, each with their own reasons just like me. The activity—all voluntary, all late at night after backbreaking daily duties were completed—stimulated whole platoons and battalions to frenzied levels of volunteer fervor. I resolved to be the most fervent and loyal volunteer of all.

In my day job, the company assigned me to the weakest unit—which meant I had the opportunity to win renown by rebuilding it. So I trained the soldiers by tying sandbags to their legs. After six months of training, their fighting power was tested again. They were tremendous in every test, including running and horizontal bar. Word got around, and they were filmed as the standard that every unit should strive to meet.

One day, I saw a broken brick in the flower beds. So I asked those who were teaching ornamentation skills to come and fix it, filling it with cement and some decorations. When the unit commissar came to inspect the premises, he was so surprised by the neat and tidy environment. Why, even the bricks in the flower bed were immaculate! The commissars asked us who was responsible for instigating this great work, but I pledged everyone to silence in order to increase the intrigue. Then six months later, I released an informant to report on my good works. Non-party-member children of deported immigrant families needed all the word of mouth they could muster if they stood any chance of joining the Communist Party.

A couple of months later, the regimental commissar told me he wanted to meet my father. So I contacted my father and brought him to the commissar. My father was more than a little surprised and cautious about being summoned to such a meeting, but I told him not to worry and just go. He brought home-brewed alcohol—the staple gift in those days. He walked into the commissar's office looking as white as a ghost. When the door opened a little while later, he exited grinning from ear to ear. "I heard you are doing very well in the military," he said with deep and obvious pride—and no small amount of relief.

After all, he was the reason why I hadn't been able to join the Communist Party in the first place. As far as the state was concerned, he was a once-exiled immigrant who had come to North Korea from China—a man of questionable loyalties, in other words. Worse yet, during the background check when I was being considered for party membership the State Security Department discovered he had visited China again. A story about illegal radios also surfaced in the investigation of my father: Next to the repair office, where my father was assigned at the time, was a person who would repair radios. One day, he mistakenly tuned into a frequency and listened to broadcasting from South Korea while my father was in the vicinity. In North Korea, even the smallest events are always noted somehow, somewhere, by someone. And they always reappear when you least want them to.

The commissar naturally needed to bring these things to the attention of my father—a gracious move, this giving the man a chance to explain things so as to clear the way for his son to go on to greater things. My father explained to him that his relatives lived in China and he of course visited there to see

46

if he could bring them to our workers' paradise. And as for the radio, he had had the opportunity to listen to the South Korean broadcasting only because of the radio mechanic's mistake. But he didn't understand the message, he added hastily, and he wasn't interested in it anyway.

The regimental commissar waved it all away with a flick of the paperwork. "Once I make up my mind," he assured my father, "I can let your son join the Communist Party any time I want." My father was undoubtedly relieved that I would not have to suffer what he had.

Shortly after that meeting, the company commander called me and said, "Hey, you'll be asked to be the management leader." When a soldier has no stripes on his shoulders, it means he is a simple soldier. Corporals get one stripe, staff sergeants get two, sergeants first class get three, master sergeants get a thick stripe, and management leaders get two thick stripes. Management leader is the highest level one can achieve before becoming an officer.

I waved off the compliment. "I'm not allowed to join the Communist Party," I said casually.

"That shouldn't be a problem," he said equally casually. *Shouldn't be a problem?*

And that is how I was promoted to the rank of management leader. I was so moved by the impossibility of it all that I cried.

I was told that everyone agreed that I should join the party. When you join the party, you need surety. If the company commander and officers want to stand as your surety, it is the highest honor. At that time, the regimental commissar himself stood up for me. Whenever others joined the party, they had opponents, but not me. Not a single person opposed my joining the Communist Party.

As a management leader, I had 120 soldiers under my command. I spent six extra months in the military, trained a replacement accordion player, and then received official military appointment to a university.

47

Well, almost. Wonsan University of Economics was the best university where the elites went, and the army was going to send me there. But then someone once again discovered my family background, and I was sent to engineering college instead. Some things follow you around forever in North Korea.

Still, what could be better than to be able to fulfill my army duty honorably, join the Communist Party, and be able to live at home with my beloved parents while I went to college? But there was one more pleasant surprise to come.

When I started college, my age was already thirty. So I was studying with very young girls—eighteen- and nineteen-year-olds in most cases—because very few girls went into the army. So I wasn't interested in any of my female classmates. But most of the professors were women—age twenty-five or so—and they were very interested in the men who had completed their military service. The college was also used as a place for teacher training. And that is how I met Mrs. Bae.

She would come to the college for these teacher training events. Never, of course, would a woman talk to a man first. So the first three times we passed each other in the hall, we just made eye contact. She had her things to do in the college, and I had my classes.

But as we passed each other each time after that, I began to ask her questions: Where do you live? How old are you? I wanted to go deeper, so I needed an excuse to build a relationship. Fortunately, the graduation requirements provided me one. In order to graduate, you needed to submit a lot of research papers. You had to write a paper about Kim Il Sung's strategy of war, and you had to write other long papers on each of eighty quotes of his—what they meant, what they meant to you, and how you would strive your whole life long to follow him. You had to have great handwriting and exactly the right answers. Then you had to write still more papers about the one hundred quotes of Kim Jong Il. Then on the top of that, you had to take a test—a comprehensive exam on all things Kim. And you had to write a thesis.

So I had a ready-made excuse to go deeper. I didn't know whether she was a good writer, but I knew I needed the help. So I asked, and she said yes. When a single North Korean woman sees a single North Korean man, they always see if the man is a party member and whether he is finished with army service. A man who did not complete army service is a man who must have bad health. A man who completed army service as a Communist Party member is a man whose family background must be okay and hasn't had any theft or women problems. And a man who completed his military service, joined the party, and enrolled in college? Only rare men would be sent to college—most men would be sent to the mines or to the factory to work, even if they were Communist Party members. So a college man like that would be very popular indeed—the right kind of a man to say yes to when he asks for help with his graduation homework.

She was not the first woman I had met. In fact, I had said no to fifty-seven women who had been recommended to me over three years. Most men who finish army duty get married within a year, but not me. After having worked so hard for so long to reverse the fortunes of our family, I was not about to risk a bad marriage. And there was something different about this woman.

She agreed to help me with my graduation papers, and I gave her one month to get my assignments done. But she sent a letter two weeks later letting me know that the papers were complete. I made arrangements to visit her home to pick them up. We ate lunch together with her parents, and afterward I examined the papers. I was absolutely blown away. She was a great writer, and everything about the papers was flawless.

My major was engineering. In order to graduate, I had to complete an engineering assignment too. I could do numbers and planning and drawing, but the writing part was beyond me. And of course I wanted to get closer to her and build our relationship. So I asked her for help on this additional assignment, and she readily agreed. And her parents liked me. Many guys had been introduced to her, she said, but none were as good as me.

In order to get that final assignment done, I went to her two-room house. Her parents stayed in one room, and we worked on the assignment in the other. We only had time in the evening, after work and school. We worked together three days, until 1:00 or 2:00 a.m. each time. That gave us time to talk too. She told me how so many of the guys who were interested in her had tried to hold her hand, but she noted that I didn't. I only focused on the task. She said that convinced her that my character was good.

On that third day, when we completed the assignment, there was no longer any pretext left for us to get together. So I asked her if she had anyone in mind for marriage. It was the first time I had openly raised the subject. She said no, she had no one in mind. So I asked her if anyone had been introduced to her by her parents, and she said no one that she was interested in. She asked me the same things. I said no.

And then I proposed right away. "I really want to think about marriage with you."

"I'm not against it," she said.

Each of us talked to our parents, and the matter was set. I met her in February—graduation month—and we married in May, three months later.

At that time, all the students who graduated from college or university were immediately sent to the most important projects the nation was undertaking—atomic power stations, fertilizer production plants, or factories of various kinds. Newspapers and television reports trumpeted the successes of each project, but those of us who worked there knew better. I was assigned to a factory project for eight years. The problems I saw there mirrored the problems our nation was having as a whole. The Great Leader died. The Soviet Union collapsed. It was as if the will of the country—not to mention its electricity and food and the last vestiges of its compassion—were sucked completely outside of its borders.

When I completed the factory project, I found a job in my hometown in the mid-1990s. At that time, all distribution had ground to a halt. That meant that although you worked, you didn't get paid. The dark shadow of famine brooded over nearly every city, village, and family. Many times I passed by the apartment where we had lived until we were exiled to the countryside. Now our starvation had followed us back even to this place. One day, the child of a neighbor died. The next evening, it was the neighbor on the back side of our home— an old woman, who slumped lifeless, starved to death in her own home. It is a very somber thing to see a dead person. I had never encountered it before in my whole life, even while in the military. And now dead bodies were everywhere—absolutely everywhere. Dead bodies on the street. Dead bodies in the houses and apartments all around us. Dead bodies piled up at the train station. One time I went to the station to catch a train. I had to wait there about an hour. Eighty orphaned children were huddled together for warmth. Seven of them were dead. Kotjebi, we call such children—worthless swallows. Dead birds. Children whose parents had died and who had nowhere to go because no one would give them anything. No one could give them anything. No one had anything to give. I could not help but remember my own starvation as a boy as I watched the station attendant chase the living children away so he could throw away the dead bodies. Worthless swallows.

I made a decision at that time: I should work in a job outside of manufacturing and construction. If you worked in manufacturing and construction, you ended up dead. There was no money to be paid to workers in those professions, and no money meant no food, which meant starvation. Fortunately, my education and party membership afforded me some options.

Since 1980 there had been a campaign to earn foreign money and bring it into the country. Of course people did this illegally on the black market all the time. But people of the highest rank could be tasked by the government with earning foreign money legally. And at the time of the famine, this was the only money to be had. So this is how I entered the world of international trade.

Of course, "international trade" in North Korea mainly means doing business with China—selling different kinds of North Korean vegetables and mineral ore. North Korea is a mountainous land, nearly impossible to farm on the top—as I had learned painfully in my childhood—but abundant in mineral resources underground. These are dug up by all the soldiers who are sent to the mines when they complete their military service. And they are sold to China as raw ore by soldiers like me who were fortunate enough to be able to go on to college. It is all sold right out of the ground to China and Russia and such places because there is no electricity and no skill to refine the ore into a higher grade. It is a sad matter.

It was a sad matter of a different sort, however, that ultimately collapsed in upon our family, which had by then grown to include our two children. Through my position in the party and my education and my work in international trade, we could stave off the famine. But through all the changes in my life, there was one thing that I had inherited from my grandparents and my parents that I never could leave behind: our family's own peculiar raw ore, which even then I had little ability to refine.

I knew little about that mysterious faith of my grandfather, and I knew even less about that mysterious God of his who had called him by name in the times of the troubles of his own people. But when my best friend, who was struggling in his marriage, asked my wife and me how we managed to live a happy life, I could not help but to tell him the truth. "There are Ten Commandments," I told him. "And heaven is always watching. When you break them, you ask heaven for forgiveness. And when you receive food, you give thanks."

It was apparently not enough to repair the struggle in his own marriage. Generally, it's not legal to get divorced in North Korea, and the process is very difficult. You have to offer proof that the person you are divorcing is quite a bad fellow. If that bad fellow is someone known to be standing against the Communist ideology—well, a society has to have priorities, you know.

And that is how I ended up going to prison for bearing the name of God. It was odd that it all happened so close to the place where the NIS had barged in so many years before. And in many ways, the whole process of investigation wasn't much different than what I remembered experiencing in my childhood—only this time there would be no going home at the end of the daily interrogation. It was clear from the beginning that I would never be going home again at all.

Those who were closest to me were also dragged in for investigation. Some of them lied about me, telling the State Security Department agents whatever they wanted or needed to hear. But who could blame them? Who needed trouble with the state?

My crime was far worse than selling illegal watches or trafficking opium, however. I had corrupted my friend through my religious "superstitions," which was the worst of political crimes. As an international trader, I was especially suspect—not only must I have been pocketing money that rightly belonged to the state, but I must also have been undermining the state with my criticisms.

Evangelism. Embezzlement. Treason. This was a trio of allegations that only had one outcome: death by execution. What ensued was, as near as I have been able to gather from those around me at the time and those North Korean defectors with whom I have spoken since, something without parallel in North Korean judicial history: more than a year in the harshest prison conditions without formally being charged while the government investigated the case.

I was treated like an insect in prison. Every day of those thirteen months was the same. Up at 5:00 a.m. Mop the floor. Clean up. Go to the restroom. Throw out the contents of the bucket. Then I had to sit cross-legged with my hands on my knees in the same position for the next seventeen hours. I was not permitted to turn my neck or slouch with my back. Every two hours, we were allowed to urinate. The only other time we were allowed to move was during meals, which were exactly one minute long. At 10:00 p.m., we were allowed to go to bed, but our heads had to be turned away from the prison bars. "Bed" meant laying down on the wooden floor.

When you're sitting, you cannot move, even if you get bit by a mosquito. If you even flinch, you receive punishment—torturous humiliations dreamed up by the guards. In one punishment, you'd have to stand with your knees bent, holding a full bowl of water over your head for thirty minutes. If you spilled even a drop, you'd be beaten senseless with a rod. For another punishment, you had to extend your hands through the prison bars so the guard on the other side could mash your palms into bloody ribbons of flesh with a sharp iron spike. You might be ordered to hang from a bar for half an hour or crawl like an insect across the wooden floor.

Mostly, though, I just sat, unmoving, for seventeen hours a day, for more than a year of my life. And during that time, I came to think a lot about my life and all that I had experienced to that point. I thought about how, during my army duty, I had buried God's love in a back room of my heart and instead received love from my superiors. I thought about how I had sought admission to the Communist Party above everything else in life, how I had come home pridefully when I achieved this. I thought about going to college and graduating and getting a job that paid money even in the midst of the famine, and how I had kept my family safe owing, I thought at the time, to my intelligence and hard work, even though so many others had starved to death. I thought about all the conversations I had had with my parents in those years after I came back from the military, and how everything they had shared with me had fallen on deaf ears. I thought about how I had forgotten God and failed to rely on him. I thought about how I had relied only on my own brilliance.

And as I came to look back on it all, I also remembered the Sundays at my grandfather's house and the question and answer sessions in the shadow of the pine trees along the beach. Hananim!...

And this is how I came to repent for the shortcomings of my faith, for not receiving fully and passing on completely all that my grandparents and parents had treasured more than party membership, more than singing contests, more than athletic medals, more than life.

And so sitting there hour after hour, day after day, month after month, as one year yielded to its successor, I repented. And of all things, a spirit of thankfulness rose up in me. I became thankful to the Lord for this time in prison—his arresting me from my own pride and drawing me into a time of reflecting, of mumbling too soft for words, of striving to remembering by his grace every hymn that we had ever sung, every lesson my grandfather had ever taught. That is how I came to rely on only the Holy Spirit with faith.

"For everyone who asks receives; the one who seeks finds; and to the one who knocks, the door will be opened"—I kept recalling that scripture. My mother used to whisper it to me on so many nights in the windy, frigid, rugged mountain village of our exile when hunger gripped us with its dull ache and hope eroded like the field we farmed. Hananim!... I called his name in my head thousands of times over, and then a thousand thousands yet again.

And God did not abandon me. In fact, quite to the astonishment of everyone, he saved me. Usually, the authorities would hand down their ruling within a month. But if your crime was particularly bad, you could pass the preliminaries in one to three months before being sent to a concentration camp or publicly executed, mouth stuffed with rocks. Once the investigation was complete, if you were called to come out and go home, it meant you were going to die. That's what "go home" meant. Almost no one left the prison alive; ninety-nine percent of them received judgment and paid the penalty.

But after more than a year, I was released as an innocent man. I was never charged at all. My past record had been examined, my accounts scrutinized, my associates interrogated. And in the end, no weapon formed against me was able to prosper. A case like mine had never happened in the history of the department. All the staff there were astonished. I came to experience God's working; something human power can neither control nor comprehend.

After I was released from prison, I was even given the opportunity to return to my job in international trade. I had a lot of questions about our faith for my mother that had piled up during my season of reflection and repentance in prison. I asked her a lot of things about the Bible, how to pray over the meal like Grandfather used to do, and how to gather on Sunday and keep the day holy. My mother had a new believer tract for me. She had risked her life to bring it back from China where she had visited a church there. I came to have a faith life.

So if you were to ask me how you can be a Christian and yet bow down before the statues of Kim Il Sung and Kim Jong Il, my answer now would be: you can't, once your faith life is awakened inside. I studied the Ten Commandments intently, one by one. I felt how much of a vain life I had lived so far in my idolatry of Kim Il Sung and Kim Jong Il, a soldier bowing down to their statues and pledging my life to their portraits and crying out to their pictures. You can't.

Our family didn't know every scripture of the Bible, but we knew enough to stop attending the idolatrous events where, on Kim Il Sung's birthday, people go to his statue and bow down and worship. And we didn't attend voting either. Instead, we followed the Ten Commandments, giving food to our neighbors, who were going through difficult times and starving to death on the streets. We respected our parents. We didn't lie. And we kept the Lord's day.

These things are easier said than done in North Korea, I can tell you that. But I think it must be true of every Christian in every country in every faith life, isn't it? Don't steal. Don't covet. Don't lie. Honor your mother and father. If we do these things from our hearts, is there a city on earth—or an apartment, or a rocky village farm—where we will truly be at home?

In North Korea, we were presented with a peculiar choice: commit idolatry every waking moment, or commit a capital offense by refusing to commit idolatry. Would you wear the Kim Il Sung button required to be worn by every citizen, or would you wear the uniform of the concentration camp? Would you send your children to school to teach them to worship Kim Il Sung, or would you march them off to the concentration camp? Would you send your son to the military to give his whole body to the worship of the Great Leader, or would you fill his mouth with rocks before the firing squad of soldiers? It was not unlike my mother's having to choose between stealing and suicide. And I had already been sent to prison for small faith, and yet I had been released. What was I to do now that my faith was in full flower?

Sometimes you must leave your village and your people in order to save them; my grandfather's God had told him once, long ago. And no one will understand as you leave everything you have ever received and known and loved as you follow the voice of that mysterious God and walk slowly but resolutely out of town.

3. MOTHER:
Vending the Bread of Life

From Mr. Bae

When a fellow teacher told my mom one day that a man had stopped to visit her while she was busy teaching, my mom's heart began pounding.

Thankfully, this visit was social; it did not entail security agents and barking dogs and beaten-down doors. It was how my mother met my father.

Both my parents were born into devout Christian families in China. My maternal grandparents attended a different church than my paternal grandparents did, but they shared the same resolve—that their children would marry other Christians from families that they knew. My maternal grandmother was close to one of the church members whose son—my future father—was a teacher at the school where her daughter—my future mother—also taught. Even though they were at the same school, my parents didn't know each other before their families began to discuss the possibility of marriage. My father didn't even know what my mother looked like or which teacher she was. He hadn't even seen her picture. But fortunately for him she was very pretty.

When my mother went out to meet my father for the first time, she went with her two friends. My dad stood very tall at five feet eleven, while my mom was only four eleven. Initially, my mom didn't find him attractive because she thought he was too tall for her. But she was attracted to his intelligence and masculinity. So they told their parents their opinions of each other and finally got married.

The Cultural Revolution propelled my parents and most of my family members out of China and into North Korea. For my parents, it also propelled them out of the classroom and into work at a North Korean snack and candy factory. After all, they were immigrants, and immigrants could not be entrusted with the important work of teaching. So they made snacks and candy instead. Because my mom was very attractive, the guys at work would often come on to her. But my mom didn't even so much as glance at any of them. She was my dad's.

It wasn't until they moved into my grandparents' house in my grandparents' later years that my parents began to live out their faith in God. They started by praying before meals and keeping the Sabbath.

I used to go along with my mother to many places. One day, my mom asked my grandfather if he would accompany us on a walk. She couldn't talk freely in the house for fear that it had been bugged. At that time, in 1970, the government was on a campaign to exterminate all Christians, so believers were very careful to take precautions against bugging devices.

My mom asked my grandfather, "Dad, did you really hear God's voice?" When he told her yes, she pressed him for all the details. He shared how God's voice was especially clear to him when he fasted, prayed, or slept. My mom told him that she'd like to hear God as he had heard. She was sad that she couldn't hear God, wondering how much deeper her dad's faith was than hers.

At that time, she was in her thirties and curious about her faith. She kept asking him about Noah's Ark, Sodom and Gomorrah, and the way people were created. Because there were no Bibles at that time in North Korea, her father became her living Bible. And she learned well. After he died, she passed those Bible stories on to me, all from memory. That's how we came to know the Ten Commandments and a few hymn songs too.

After my grandfather died and we were exiled to live in the farming area, we didn't pray before meals. Too dangerous, my mom said. But she still gathered us children together, often overnight, to give us lessons just like my grandfather had given her and her siblings each week—that we should live in accordance with the Ten Commandments and that we should remember what happened to Sodom and Gomorrah. She told us stories about Moses too—how his mother placed him in a basket and put it among the reeds along the bank of the Nile. It was fun to hear her tell us these old stories, but her purpose was never to entertain. The point was always the same, especially when we were going through the hardest times: God always watches us wherever we are, and he sees whatever we do. She wanted us to remember that, and she wanted us not to sin.

We had a hard life in the barren farming village. There were many times when my dad blamed my mom for our circumstances because she had invited the Chinese criminal into our home. But, my mom would say, "How can we of all people ignore those poor people who come here from China? How can we, as Christians, live like that? It might be a test from God. We should always live out our faith every moment and never let it be shaken." Dad accepted what she said, but he didn't like it.

Still, she always lived out her faith. She had compassion for the hungry and poor, sharing her few possessions with them. She was always considerate and generous to people. And during those hard times, she encouraged all of us—my dad, myself, and my siblings.

While Dad easily became annoyed and started arguments when he was having difficulty, Mom didn't change even a bit. She overcame each difficulty with a smile. Though she was short, she wasn't afraid of anything. "Why am I supposed to be afraid of anything?" she asked. "God is on my side, and he'll make a way for us. Even in the hard times, he'll solve all our problems. But why should we focus on the difficulties?" When she had moved to North Korea from China (which was a crime—smuggling), she wasn't afraid at all. She genuinely believed God would keep her safe.

My mom was wise too. She was even a pioneer in business in North Korea. She had no training in this area, but necessity makes a good teacher when God is your coach. Let me explain.

When we were exiled to the farming area, Mom raised the children while Dad worked in a factory and did the farmwork. She gave birth to three more children during that time and, by the time we left the farming area, there were six of us siblings. Because Dad worked manual labor, we received food rations from the government, but—since we were immigrant offenders—never as much as we were supposed to. Our allotment was 700 grams a day, but we always received 550, less than what is necessary to sustain life. The rest was always skimmed off the top by the government, who required that every family "donate" part of their rice allotment to the government's "war fund."

As a result, Mom did something that had, so far as any of us know, never been done before anywhere in Communist North Korea. She became an independent businesswoman—a bread vendor. She knew nothing about baking bread or running a business. All she knew was that her children should grow up healthy and that God would guide and protect her to accomplish that godly desire.

Personal vendors like her were, of course, illegal in a Communist country, but Mom found a very clever way to make it work, with the full cooperation of the government. In North Korea, a feeding and clothing manager manages several state-operated restaurants. Mom brokered a deal whereby she would report all her baking sales to the manager and then give half of the money she made to the restaurant while keeping the other half. Everyone won—the government, the manager, and Mom's children, who didn't die. In fact, we grew up quite healthy given the circumstances.

She was good at making bread too. By adding about 5 percent flour to the corn rice, the bread came out absolutely delicious. She had never been taught how to make bread before, so she made it her own way—like fried pancakes on an iron skillet. Some restaurant customers would order ten loaves of her bread!

This early exercise in creative entrepreneurship would prove crucial twenty years later. That's because by the time 1990 rolled around, government rations were dwindling down to nothing, but government zeal for arresting vendors was on the rise. They only allowed people to sell items they could make or grow or gather for themselves—things like bush clover, sticks, and dustpans. If a vendor was caught selling clothes or shoes or bread, he or she would be arrested on suspicion of having stolen from the government's supply.

So my mom used her brains again. Or, more accurately, she prayed—though you might not recognize that if you saw her, because North Korean Christians can't bow their heads or close their eyes like you can. If they do, they will end up in jail or in a concentration camp. So what I saw when I would wake up in the middle of the night was my mom, quietly sitting still for long stretches of time, listening for the voice of the One that had thundered out so many times to her father.

That is how she came up with the idea to buy imported items from China and sell them to our neighbors. This new work wasn't illegal: We were from China, after all, and we had relatives there. There was no law against selling what your relatives sent from China.

Even though there were others selling Chinese goods, a lot of people bought from us. My mom would promote the goods by pointing out that ours were less expensive than others since we received the goods directly from our relatives in China.

At that time, a surprising new policy was introduced in North Korea, handed down by Kim Jong Il himself. No longer would the government provide rations, the Dear Leader announced. Instead, people would henceforth have to provide for themselves. Somehow people would have to solve on their own their need to eat, while also making money for transportation and fuel.

Fortunately, my parents were well equipped for the task. Their foreigner skills, so long a source of pain and loss, finally paid off: they were excellent Chinese speakers in a country where few citizens could speak Chinese. My mom had an old friend in China whose son was running a trading company, so they visited in hopes of my father hiring on as an interpreter. They impressed this Chinese family by making them laugh with a joke told entirely in Chinese. More important, they explained how there was nothing illegal about what my parents were proposing. That sealed the deal: the family secured an employment certificate for my dad, and my parents moved to the China/North Korea border in the early 1990s—just in time once again for God to save our family and to use us to save the lives of many. My grandfather's story was continuing—through us!

Being an interpreter for a trade company provided the perfect opportunity for my father to travel in and out of North Korea in order to disciple the company's partners. Because the company's partners were being discipled by him, they made favorable reports about him to the government. The whole time my mom guided him, directing him to send nearly all the money he made to us children.

And the goal was not for any of us to get rich. As always, my mom's focus was on helping the poor. She aided the North Koreans who were seeking to escape from all the hunger and suffering. This was even before the March of Tribulation—the new and unparalleled level of starvation and suffering that began in 1995. Since my mom was known as someone who was willing to help others, orphans also visited her asking for money. Mom always helped them with a warm heart. Soon, their house was crowded and noisy with people seeking help. Mom didn't complain at all about this, but some family members were worried that she might get in trouble with the government for harboring troublemakers. But she chided us, "Do you think that you caused your well-being on your own? We truly owe everything to God. Everything we have has been given to us by God."

In saying this, she once again refocused us on God in the midst of a difficult time. No one needed that refocusing more than my little brother. My parents got cheated many times by those who visited their house, so he became resentful and often shook his finger at Mom. She liked me because I didn't behave like him.

At that time, my mom decided that it wasn't enough for the poor to eat a meal at their house and just leave, so she made up her mind to send them to churches in China for further help. She counseled orphans to head to China and look for a building with a cross on top. "Say you're from North Korea and ask to live there," she said, knowing that the churches would take them in. As the world crumbled in famine around her, even when it became hard for my mom to look after herself, she daily undertook the dangerous work of directing North Korean people to Chinese churches. She was especially protective of pretty girls who had nothing to eat. In China, the shortage of women coupled with the sheer human desperation of the famine condemned them almost certainly to the sex trade. So she would always give them to same instructions: Go to China to a building with a cross on top, get married, and keep going back to that building with the cross.

Even as she entered old age, my mom didn't have any health problems. Her eyesight didn't fade, and she could still hear well. And one voice was unmistakable for her—it was the one her father had heard that she had longed to hear too. I don't know that she ever heard it quite the way he did, but I know she did something that he never did: she began to evangelize as many North Koreans as she could.

And it wasn't just her family members that she reached. Sensing the end of her days approaching, she intensified her efforts to awaken for Christ every North Korean she met. Moreover, she went back and forth to China picking up materials for new believers and smuggling them back inside North Korea. These were usually palm-sized thin books that could be concealed, though smuggling them was always dangerous. She would wrap them in vinyl and hide them in different places around the house to avoid detection in the event of a search.

I shake my head in amazement as I reread what I just wrote. I wish I could convey to you how impossible this work was, and how my mom did it with absolutely no fear. She evangelized her neighbors—this simply never happens in North Korea. Nobody would dare evangelize neighbors—too many spies. Everyone is ordered to report all that they've seen in the lives of those around them. They spy on one another too, trying to figure out whether the other is really a spy or not. Jesus said wherever two are three are gathered together in his name, there he is. But in North Korea wherever two or three are gathered together, they will always doubt the identity of the others and wonder which one is a government spy. How could anyone evangelize in this situation?

My mom did. If I recall correctly, about seven people visited her house at different times. My mom would march them into the room, lock the door, and study new believer's materials together with them. They would emerge from that room saved and depart as fellow believers. It was simply amazing. First, the bread business. Next, the import business. Now, this. Who can understand what a pioneer my mother was in North Korean society?

She always told us to move to China. In North Korea, my younger sister and brother were teachers. You can't imagine how hard it is to work as a teacher in North Korea. They have no choice but to eat porridge for every meal, and even then, they hardly ever get enough to eat. Worse yet, can you imagine being an underground Christian teaching in an education system built entirely around the glorification and worship of Kim Il Sung and Kim Jong Il?

But my younger sister and my sister-in-law were paralyzed with fear and afraid to do anything. In fact, their solution to our family's challenges was to urge my mom to turn herself in to the authorities. If Mom got caught, all of us would be sent to a concentration camp for her "crimes." So my sister and sister-in-law wanted Mom to confess her activities and exonerate the rest of family. But Mom was unwavering. She said, "The world will come to an end within several years. Before then, I need to evangelize as many people as I can. So don't ask me to turn myself in."

But Mom had my attention when she urged all of us to move to China. As time had gone on and I had grown in my faith, the idolatry of North Korean society increasingly troubled my conscience. How could we worship God and obey the Ten Commandments in that environment? Meanwhile, more laws were instituted to curb "dissent." Women were only permitted to wear skirts when going out. The heels of their shoes had to be shorter than 5 cm. People were forbidden to wear shirts with English writing on them. Long hair was criminalized. Electricity, rations, and train service were no longer provided.

These were not simply peculiar inconveniences: our daughter was interrogated overnight when she wore pants outside the house one day, and we could do nothing to inquire about her whereabouts or determine how we could help. Given the intense scrutiny we were under due to my past, every new law provided the government with one more pretext to examine and detain us. The net was closing fast. Would it be days, weeks, or months until my mother was apprehended and she, along with our whole family, sent to one of North Korea's concentration camps?

But that wasn't the main reason I thought to leave. It was a memory. I remembered back to the time when, as a child, I accompanied my mother to walk with my grandfather and she asked, "Did you actually hear God's voice?" She had so longed for a faith deep enough to hear God speak, and now, here she was, standing on the brink of imprisonment, absolutely fearless, proclaiming the Word of God. It reminded me of Grandfather standing in the door of the church, blocking the advance of the Japanese. She had become like him.

And me? As I stood on the threshold of the most important decision of my life, I remembered God's call to my grandfather to leave behind everything in his village in order to save it. And I knew I had become like them too, through their teaching and example and by the grace of God. I would leave everything and follow God, in order to save everything that I held dear and knew I could not save on my own. So I decided to leave North Korea and go not only to China but all the way to South Korea. By God's grace I would make a way for my whole family to follow, in the hope that one day, we could save our people too.

The moment I turned to cross the river into China, my mother called just one phrase after me.

"Keep the faith."

4. WIFE:

An Altogether Different Kind of Paratrooper

From Mrs. Bae

My father was a business inspector for the government, and my mother was a government worker. Frankly, I did not know a thing about politics as a child. What I did know, however, was that our family had a strong tradition of integrity. Looking back on it, my husband and I think my parents probably knew a lot about politics and how to stay out of trouble and in the good graces of the government.

But even then, the law was unnecessary to them. Though they were workers for the economy, they never stole things or sold them on the black market like so many workers did. Instead, they always did extra work with every available spare moment. My father would go out to the fields at 3:00 a.m. before his day job. My mother and grandmother took in extra sewing and weaving. As a result, though we were a family of twelve, we never lacked for food, and all our neighbors envied our happiness. We ate well, dressed well, and lived comfortably. Education was free for all when I entered school in 1969.

I think that when I was an elementary school student, my siblings and I grew up well, not because of the moral education from the school, but simply because we watched how my parents lived. The ethical education from the school was all about greeting everyone well, not stealing from others, and so on. But my parents would never have let us do harm to others or allow us to talk behind someone's back, anyway.

My parents' moral education had a much higher standard. They used to say, "You cannot give to other people if you eat whatever you want." They taught us that when you give something to someone else, give enough. For example, when most people shared food with their neighbors, they would usually only give a little bit—just enough so they could take credit for being generous. My parents were different. When they made *songpyeon* (a half-moon-shaped rice cake), not only was it delicious, but they always made more than was needed. That way, everyone in our family could have some and also have enough to give to neighbors. My parents wanted their neighbors to really enjoy the songpyeon. They taught us like that.

My siblings lived near the ocean. Sometimes they brought fish and seafood to us. My parents told us to give some of the fish and seafood to the neighbors, and they wouldn't allow us to give away the worst of it. My mother always checked the fish and seafood that we prepared. Then she would say, "You should be ashamed to give like that! Give them better." That is how I learned from my parents. I learned more from them than from school.

And because I lived under my parents' refinement and teaching, I received a lot of praise in school. My classmates voted to award me the prestigious Knocking Bird's Egg badge in second grade. I received the highest rank in the class: top class president. Our class had fifty-six students. The class was divided into groups of six or seven students. A class president took care of a small group of six to seven students. But the top class president took care of all fifty-six students and was given a special tie to wear.

I learned how to write earlier than others too. As an inspector, my father was often away on business trips. Once, after he had returned from a business trip, he was watching me quietly as I was doing my homework. I was writing a report after reading just a few pages. My father said, "You are very smart. How could you memorize and write that many sentences after just reading the material one time?" I guess I had a pretty good memory. I could read a page one time and know it well enough to be able to copy it without looking. Actually, my parents were very smart too.

The school did not systematically teach me how to read, speak, and write, but in my role as a top class president, I learned to do those things. In North Korea, speech contests are held often. I took part in these contests and won many first prizes. The speeches had titles like "Punishing Americans," "Cracking Down on America," "America is the Mortal Enemy of North Korea," and "Americans' Brutality toward North Korea during the Korean War."

Even in elementary school, they taught us about the great, then head of state, Kim Il Sung. North Korean education is based on how faithful you are to the Great Leader. So the first thing I learned at school was, "Great Leader Kim Il Sung, thank you!" Every hour, the purpose of class was to study our obligation to the revolution. Regardless of what we were learning—whether it was the Korean alphabet or calculation— the entire purpose of the education was to train students to serve as revolutionary soldiers who would forever be faithful to Kim Il Sung. We were taught that Kim Il Sung was God and that we would die without him—we would starve to death, our nation would be invaded, and we would become slaves of America or Japan. In order to guard our nation and Kim Il Sung, we had to do well in school and life. That was the main purpose of our education. And as revolutionary soldiers, we had to learn useful and practical knowledge.

I was certainly among the most faithful of students. In elementary school, I received commendations on three different occasions: one from the military, one from the Young

Adult Alliance, and one from a government official. I was the top student in the whole school of eight hundred students.

I certainly didn't grow up as a Christian, but that doesn't mean I never heard about Christianity. Here is one of the stories I learned about an American missionary from my textbooks.

The story happened before the Homeland Liberation War, or what you call the Korean War. The story is that there was a housekeeper who worked for an American missionary. The name of the housekeeper's son was Bok-Nam. Bok-Nam came to the missionary's home to look for his mother. The house was surrounded by a fence, and an apple from a tree in the missionary's yard had fallen outside of the fence. Bok-Nam picked up the apple, and the son of the missionary saw it. The son of the missionary came home and said, "Father, Bok-Nam stole our apple!"

Then, the missionary brought Bok-Nam in his house and carved the word "Thief" on Bok-Nam's forehead. In acid.

"But the missionary was the real thief," our textbook taught us. The missionary wore the mask of a sheep but was really a hypocrite who stole into North Korea. He was wicked on the inside, we learned.

The government taught us like that in order to prevent us from believing in Jesus. What I realized is that North Korea used the Homeland Liberation War to convince North Koreans to hate America, and they used the story of the missionary to cause us to reject God.

They also taught us that the missionary tried to teach North Koreans a "stupid" culture. How foolish it was, they said, that if someone strikes you on the cheek, you should turn to him the other also. A nation would fall that way, which they said was exactly the missionary's goal.

So from childhood, every North Korean student was taught to worship Kim Il Sung and him alone. As far as we knew, there was no other god.

An elementary school in North Korea has four grades. After elementary school, North Korean children enter into a secondary school, or middle-high school. The middle-high school has six grades. Preschool is available for a year prior to elementary school but is optional.

When students turn nine years old, they can join the Youth Party League. The necktie is their badge. Youth Party League must take an oath in order to enter. After taking the oath, students who do well at secondary school are given a tie. I was the first student in my class to become a Youth Party League and be awarded a tie—quite an accomplishment for a girl!

After graduating from elementary school, I entered into secondary school. I did well there because I studied hard. I did not like falling behind other students. As I look back on it, I think God gave me wisdom at that time. That must be how I succeeded.

I was good at writing. My handwriting was neat, and I was also good at writing compositions. My most memorable moment was when I wrote an essay called "A Day of Hiking," which won first prize in a contest. At that time, my older brother was in the graduating class. He said to me, "Your teacher said that you are the best. So, let's test it." Then, my brother gathered his friends around and asked me to write something right there on the spot that he would read. And I did. "Wow! You are really good," he said.

We learned physics, chemistry, and biology. Students would prepare thick reports on experiments, and then teachers would grade them. After grading, they allowed only the most qualified students to take an exam; the rest could not. Students treated it like a competition. I worked really hard. I tried to make my reports look as professional as possible. Students had to make them by themselves, since parents were always kept too busy to help. Fortunately, since childhood, I had read many books, and I knew how I could make book covers look nicer. My favorite memories from my school days all involve reading books and writing.

Schools announced the results of each contest in public. Whenever I won second place, I would be crushed, unable to sleep. Whenever I won first place, I would sleep comfortably— the satisfied rest of the student revolutionary.

In secondary school, I was the top class president from first grade to third grade. Male students felt uncomfortable with me because I did not talk much and my talent was outstanding, I had leadership skills, and I often participated in activities like the speech contests. Actually, come to think of it, both male and female students felt uncomfortable with me.

Still, I was kindhearted due to the guidance of my parents. There were many students who were not doing well at all in school and many who were hopeless because of difficult situations. They had to rely on food rations, and if their parents were jobless or sick, life was really bad for them. I helped them a lot when I was the top class president. When I organized groups, I matched good students with poor students. Sometimes I collected firewood and shared it with needy students. I also asked students who had extra money to donate it to needy students. I even asked each student to collect pocket money for the poor students. If there was a student who did not have shoes, notebooks, or pencils, I gave mine or asked other students to share theirs. At lunchtime, I gathered every student who could not afford to bring food and encouraged other students to share their lunch with them.

In those days, this was not an easy thing to do in North Korea. Frankly, there were not many people who performed good deeds; however, I did—because of the education from my parents. My father taught me to be kind and gracious to others. He taught me to go and greet even those pushing farmers' carts. I watched and saw how he would warmly hail them, "Brother, where do you come from?" That was the role model we saw. There were hunchbacks in my town too, and they always suffered from discrimination and public neglect. Not at my parents' table, though—my parents' cooking was great, and there was always room even in our large family for hunchbacks to come eat with us on special days.

So far I've shared with you all the things I was good at. But there is one thing I was definitely *not* good at—shooting a gun. When I was in fourth grade in secondary school, I joined a young adult military club. I was very timid. There were a couple of male students who shot bull's-eyes every time they pulled the trigger. I never even hit the target. Every bullet I shot flew off into the mountains.

But the thing I hated most was what we called "the battle of village farm support." From secondary first grade to third grade, we had to go to the village farm after school to work. Once we reached fourth grade, we received a sort of food stamp as part of the food rationing system. Children would go to the workplaces of their parents to get a food stamp good for fifteen days or a month. Then we would take it to wherever we had to in order to get the food ration, usually the village farm. People usually went out to the farm at 5:00 a.m., before their main job, in order to work the field for their rations, but kids couldn't go that early because it is too cold outside. Even May is very cold in North Korea; if it rains or is even cloudy, it is usually too cold for kids to work on the farmland.

At the village farm, each household was responsible for their own area, which was about 350 square feet. You scoop out rice seedlings all day long by yourself, and for that day's labor, you receive 0.5 points. But to receive food, you have to make one point. So imagine scooping out all the rice seedlings in a 700-square-foot area in order to receive your food ration. It was exhausting. It was hard to study *and* support the village farm *and* serve in the youth organizations. Fortunately, I did not have to work as much as others did because I was the youngest one in our family.

In the spring, we would have to spend thirty to forty-five days weeding our part of the field in the village farm. In the fall, we had fifteen days to harvest rice and corn. After the rice seedlings matured, we would have to scoop them out and transfer them to the rice paddies by hand. I really hated it.

In secondary school, loyalty to the state was absolutely fundamental. On top of everything else, each student had to plant beans and hand in at least a couple of pounds every year. We also had to collect scrap iron, glass, and bottles and hand those in too.

One of the most difficult assignments for students was to hand in rabbit skins. We each had to raise a rabbit at home, eat it, and hand in the skin. Trouble was, no family members would help me take care of the rabbit. I complained to my parents about it, but my brother and sister had to have skins too. And the school didn't take small skins. I really did not like to do those tasks.

The school would send all the supplies we collected to the military or to construction sites. The importance of studying is stressed to all North Korean students, but so is the importance of supporting the village farm, the importance of planting beans, the importance of collecting scrap, and the importance of skinning rabbits. So the life of the North Korean student is constant labor, both mental and physical.

Unlike the rabbit, I survived. And I even received a recommendation enabling me to go to university—one of only four students in my school to be selected. After the universities select their students, the military then recruits whoever they want from the remaining students. Those who aren't chosen end up at the mine or the village farm. In my time, that meant students followed in the footsteps of their parents: If parents went to a village farm, their kids went with them. If parents went to a mine, their kids followed them to the mine.

I was recommended for the university, but teachers also recommended me to join the military. So I took a physical examination for the military and an entrance examination for the university, simultaneously. I received a letter of acceptance from both. When I saw some of my friends entering the military, I wanted to join the military too. But my parents said,

"Your brother and sister joined the military. How can you join the military too?" My parents wanted me to be a teacher because they thought teachers never got rained or snowed on, and that the heel of the teacher's shoe would not get dirty.

But I refused to give up so easily. Prior to my father's business trips, my parents would have a meal together. So on one such occasion, I opened the door, strode into the room where they were eating, and announced, "Only reactionaries are living here. I will join the military and become a paratrooper!" I had huge ambition. "I will get on a plane and become a paratrooper. Later, I will be honorably discharged from the military as a battalion commander. I will show you! I want to join the military as soon as possible!"

But they looked up at me, nonplussed. "You cannot," my father intoned. My parents insisted that a career as a teacher was most suitable for me. And so, because of their opposition to me joining the military, I had no choice but to enter the university.

Many professors wanted to have me as their student. They said, "You must come to us." They wanted me to be an elementary school teacher, a middle-high school teacher, and even a Youth Party League teacher. The Youth Party League teacher contacted my parents and asked them "What do you want your daughter to be?" My parents told him that I had to be a teacher.

I really didn't want to be a teacher. I protested to my parents, "How do I take care of little kids?" But my parents said that being a teacher was a clean job. So that's where I started my career.

One reason I didn't want to be a teacher was that in North Korea teaching always involves daily pledges of loyalty to the state, and it all gets a bit tiresome—especially for the leader. From secondary school, first grade on, students had to recite a written oath toward our respectable father, Kim Il Sung, and then classes began. As top class president of the students in my school growing up, I had to carry the oath around, always at the very front of my backpack. It was sealed with a red cover. The first page was the written oath to Kim Il Sung. The next page was another written oath that said something like, "I will study hard and do well as a Youth Party League." I had to lead them every day. So I was eager to not have to be the one to do this at the university.

Then, there was group life, all-day meetings designed to make sure that in every area of our lives, we were living as revolutionary soldiers. Groups of forty-five students would sit together during group life. The head of the college association and a teacher led each group. Originally group life would last for two days. Later, it was changed to a week. In addition, there was monthly group life, quarterly group life, and yearly group life. As a student, I had to write a daily report, a planning report, and create the meeting agendas. I really hated to do those, and I vowed to myself that I would never become a leader of a college association once I got to university.

But wouldn't you know it; I became the head of the college association at our university. I really did not like it. Every day, I had to attend to the tasks of the group-life program at dawn. I had to inspect group-life journals of students daily. As the head of the college association, I had no time for study. When others were studying, I had to write group-life reports, assign group-life grades, and develop group-life plans. I had to present my record of group life to the Committee of College Associations for inspection. While others were returning home at 6:00 p.m., I wasn't getting home until 11:00 p.m. As a result, I started to specialize in college association work rather than majoring in education.

No one thought this was the least bit odd. Even at the university, being a revolutionary soldier was fundamental. We were developing the history of the revolution, after all. We spent most of our time learning about the great policy of Communism and Socialism, so we had little time for studying much else. We all wanted to be teachers and Communist

Party members at the same time. And being admitted to the Communist Party took a lot more than skinning a few rabbits.

I graduated from the university with the ambition of party membership. I also graduated from the university with honors. And that meant that I *should* have been in line for a prestigious position at a top school.

But in North Korea, everything always comes back to the needs of the party and the state and the revolution. Since I was originally from a village very close to the North/South Korea border, that meant that I—and everyone in my village—had special responsibilities for civilian military service. So I was sent to pull guard duty protecting a mountain that was considered particularly vulnerable to attack from the South. Fortunately, my record distinguished me, and I was called back to the university and given the opportunity to complete my studies.

But after graduation, I was assigned to a school right back near the border again. From the schoolyard I could see the barbed wire of the DMZ--the Demilitarized Zone, a strip of land that serves as a buffer between North and South Korea. So much for prominence and prosperity.

Life for North Korean teachers (especially single, young, talented ones) doesn't involve a lot of consistency and stability, however. Soon, I was assigned to a school for eight months. Later, I was summoned to another city to serve at a school there. But it wasn't all bad. In fact, most people seem to recall their college years as the fondest memories of their lives. But most people didn't have to present their records of group-life meetings to the Committee of College Associations for inspection until eleven at night. So, some of the happiest memories of my young life happened in those early years of teaching. I had a lot of energy and many good ideas, I was getting better at my job, and my performance was good—even though I had to walk twenty-two miles to get to the school from downtown because I had no car. But at least there were no rabbits to skin.

When my school-on-the-border participated in sports, we were never able to win championship games, due to our small number of students. But I yelled until I was hoarse, watching volleyball, basketball, and handball.

There were many solo contests such as playing instruments or singing. I trained students in singing, harmonica, and the accordion. I trained them to win. I didn't want others to look down on our school because of its size. I told our students, "If you do not win the contest, you should die there. I do not want you to win second place. Win first, now!" It was memorable.

Because of my good performance, I attained fame. There were (and are) many awards and measurements of excellence for students and teachers. I received ten recommendation letters from others all at the same time, and the letters were reported to the school. This led to a prestigious assignment for me at an up-and-coming school, tasked with the responsibility of making sure it achieved the rare and coveted designation of "model school." No one taught me how to achieve that designation, however. I had to figure it all out on my own and do the paperwork by myself. The process was hopelessly complex. There were criteria that had to be met like how many textbooks had to be read by the students, what classes should be taught, what should be in the school's business plan, and so on.

These model school applications are always reported to the military. If the military approves them, they are reported to state government officials and reviewed for approval. After their approval, the applications are sent to a central government official. And after that, they are reviewed by the three hundred–member Central Committee of the Communist Party. So when a school is designated as a model school, it signifies that the school has the best students who are perfectly trained in body, knowledge, and morals. It benefits both the students and the teachers, but the principal of the school earns the greatest benefit.

The young female teacher who does all the hard work enabling the school and its principal to achieve the designation, however, receives nothing. Well, that's not entirely accurate. I received the undying (and completely unwanted) attention of the forty-two-year-old school principal, who gushed that he had just divorced his wife and wanted to live with me. He promised me that if I slept with him, he would grant me my fondest dream: membership in the Communist Party.

I was twenty-five at that time. I wanted so badly to be a member of the party so that people would respect me. But I had not been permitted to join the party because school officials knew that if I joined the party, I would of course get married and my teaching days would be over. So the school kept stalling—until the principal came calling.

Of course I rejected his advances. I was appalled. But social rules being what they are in North Korea, I could not tell my parents that the principal wanted to sleep with me, so I abandoned my dreams of ever being able to join the party, and I told my parents I wanted to get married right away. They were more stunned than when I had told them I wanted to be a paratrooper. "What happened to you?" they asked. "You always reared up in anger when we mentioned marriage before."

So I married Mr. Bae. We went on our honeymoon, and later I bore two children. I was happy, and my life was good, like it had been under my parents. But even though I had been very successful and smart and energetic for my whole life, all I was after having babies was ill—all the time. My parents and siblings felt sorry for me. They wondered why I was getting sick and thought it might be caused from some unknown sin in my parents' past. My whole body was sick, but there wasn't a specific name for my disease.

My husband said to me, "If it is difficult to live, then pray—with two hands together." He did not even say "Lord" or "God" or explain what prayer was. He just said that I should confess what I did wrong and pray. Frankly, I thought it humorous. I thought he was being silly. I had been continuously sick, and he told me to pray—with two hands together. When I did, I was healed. It did not last forever—I would get sick again, of course, and still do—but I didn't laugh any more when I thought about praying.

Sometimes after that first healing experience I would go outside on a moonlit night and do this pray-with-two-hands-together thing. "Why am I sick?" I would ask no one in particular as I clasped my two hands together. "I have done my best to be a good person. Why am I sick, now? Can anyone heal me?" And sometimes I would be healed.

My husband said, "Do not sin." I didn't even know what "sins" were. He explained to me that lying is a sin, looking down on people is a sin, theft is a sin, and adultery is a sin. I didn't even know what adultery meant. He said that heresy is a sin too. I didn't know what that was either. I asked him what it meant, and he said it was espionage activities. Now that I think of it, I did not know many things.

But even before I had prayed with two hands together, I had lived honestly. I felt like heaven was keeping an eye on me. I could not bear malice, nor could I curse someone. I wondered whether those were sins or not too.

There were times when I would buy something and be given the wrong amount of change. I would be entitled to receive one hundred won back, but I would be given two hundred won. I always gave it back. That would be considered rank foolishness among North Koreans. But I could not bring myself to do anything wrong. My husband always taught me not to do anything wrong, and I couldn't have even if I had wanted to.

It may sound unusual to you that a husband and wife could sleep together, have babies together, do the pray-with-two-hands thing together, and still not have an in-depth conversation where the wife could ask, "What in the world are you talking about? I can't understand half of what you are saying." But it is important to understand that North Korea is unusual like that. Husbands and wives must be very careful when they speak to each other. It takes many years before they trust each other enough to speak about deep matters like faith.

People asked me how I could assist and respect my husband so well, especially given all the strange things he said to me. But my parents had taught me well. I never nagged my husband in front of his friends. We would even share a cup of water or bowl of rice so that visitors would have more to eat and not leave our home without a treat. I have always liked to treat others to a meal and to give them something when they leave. So my husband's friends liked me.

But in North Korea, one has to be extremely careful even when speaking to old friends. There is no better illustration of this than the story of how my husband was rounded up and sent to prison, all because of a single comment he made to a friend in need one day, just trying to be helpful. This friend asked us how we had a happy life. He didn't have a good relationship with his wife. It seemed that he had fallen in love with someone else when he was young. So he was not treated well by his wife, and he wanted to know how to live together without conflict. My husband said, "We can live together without conflict because God is with us in this world," and he explained the Ten Commandments. That's all it takes in North Korea to end up sitting on the cold floor of a jail for more than a year without even being formally charged.

I think that the reason God permitted my husband to be arrested at that moment is that God wanted to teach me how to pray. My husband was in prison for more than a year, but none of his family visited the state political security department to see him. I was the only one running around for my husband.

I never understood that, so one day I called my mother-in-law. She said, "He cannot be saved by man's power. Man's power is useless." My sister-in-law said the same thing. For the first time, a prayer-with-two-hands-together suddenly rushed upon my mind quite without my effort. I told my sister-in-law, "Then, we should pray."

It was very strange that I even knew to pray. I didn't even know the order or process for prayer. I was not a well-trained believer. But what I am realizing now is that prayer is not about asking God to give me this or that. I think prayer is like a wish from the center of my heart to ask God to resolve a pitiable condition. Back then, I couldn't even sleep. I stayed up worrying about the possibility of my husband being shot dead, thinking about how I might be able to save him. I didn't know how to pray, so I just kept saying, "If you exist, God, please help us. Please don't let him die. Please let him come home."

He was in prison for more than a year, not charged but yet sentenced to be executed by a firing squad; however, he was ultimately released alive!

After he was released, my mother-in-law visited us. Now that my husband was a former prisoner, it would have been much harder for us to get official permission to visit her, and it might have raised suspicions. So I was so thankful that she was able to come to see us. There was much that I wanted to share with her, and even more that I wanted to ask.

I talked to my mother-in-law about how I had been praying continuously after my husband's arrest. I told her how I thought he had been released because of my prayer. My husband and mother-in-law laughed at what I said, me not being at that point a very knowledgeable believer and all. But I still think that my husband is alive, and was released, because I prayed so hard. God did it because I was so pitiful. My sister-in-law actually started to believe me. Then, my husband believed me too. And that's when we decided to evangelize people.

My mother-in-law wanted me to understand everything about Christianity, so that's why she made the lengthy trip to come see us. "In the beginning, God created the heavens and the earth…" Even though I was ill and very tired, I still remember everything I learned from my mother-in-law. She did not allow me to go to sleep until three each morning. But I was passionate and did not drowse at all.

When she left, my mother-in-law gave me thirty thousand won. Thirty thousand won was not a lot of money, but she said she couldn't leave without giving me something. But then she gave me something of far greater value. She said, "I believe in you. I will be back later." Those are deep words in North Korea.

She couldn't carry books into and around North Korea, so she had to learn and memorize all the hymns and Gospel songs that she learned whenever she visited a certain Korean Chinese church in northeast China. She did bring me a small booklet, though. The title of the booklet was *Material for a New Believer*. On the cover of the book, a ginkgo tree was drawn. Jesus was there, and twelve disciples were sitting next to a rock. She hid the booklet inside of her underwear, smuggling it inside of North Korea in order to deliver it to me.

She also taught me how to sing the hymns and Gospel songs she had memorized. In addition, she showed me how to repent and pray. Sometimes after that, she would visit China and then come to us quickly. Sometimes she would not be able to come. But whenever she learned a couple of new hymns or Gospel songs, sooner or later she would come to my home to teach them to me. She was truly a great woman.

When my mother-in-law began sharing the Gospel with me, I don't think I sincerely had faith. But I felt like I was secured by someone. My life was difficult and complex, but I always thought that there was someone I could depend on. But when my husband was arrested, there was nobody I could lean on. Throughout my whole life, I had thought that I was very wise and brilliant and had achieved great things through leadership. I thought I was good enough. But those kinds of thoughts came because I didn't know God. I had only a Juche education. As I heard the Gospel, I came to see that all the honors and everything I had received were gifts from God. Apart from him, I had done nothing. Apart from him, I could do nothing.

Neither could my husband. Even after his release from prison, he literally could not do anything for a year. In prison, he was seated the entire time and did not use his legs for more than a year.

I once had a surgical operation. When I entered into the operating room, I was confident that I would not die. I can't quite express why, but I entered into the operation room with confidence. My husband said that he prayed a lot for me then. I said, "I prayed hard too. I prayed for a successful operation. If God exists, he will not let me die." He just laughed. I guess my faith was growing.

One day, I visited my mother-in-law's brother. His son was a professor at a college, and he had a book. It was a thick book, like an encyclopedia, and it had information about God. There was very little difference between that book and what I had learned from my mother-in-law. She had taught me about Adam and Hawa, which is Eve's name in Korean. But the book called her Eve, her English name. The book had all kinds of information in it on world politics, North Korea, South Korea, common knowledge, which river is the longest or shortest, which mountain is highest or lowest, monthly rainfall, names of presidents and their genealogy. It also covered God's creation of heaven and earth and the Ten Commandments.

Through the discipleship from my mother-in-law and books like this one, I was beginning to understand more clearly. Even though I was a new believer, I read these books and used all my gifts of memorization and study to soak it in. I became well versed. I read so much that my husband thought I was going crazy.

My mother-in-law could not visit us very often, so there was much I did not know. I began to realize that all of North Korea's ethics education was actually based on the Bible. They had simply copied and distorted what the Bible had taught about just about everything.

From that time on, my family put up a wall against the world. We didn't attend the mandatory birthday events where all North Koreans place flowers at the foot of Kim Il Sung's statue. We sang hymns, not secular songs. Of course, we could not permit other people to hear our singing, so we would go sing quietly in the big fields whenever they were empty. Every evening, we locked the door and memorized the Lord's Prayer and the Apostles' Creed. In every area of our family life, we followed not Kim Il Sung's teaching but God's Ten Commandments. We didn't know what kind of place a church would be or what a church service would be like. But every Sunday, we would gather and memorize the Apostles' Creed, sing hymns, pray along with the Lord's Prayer, and repent according to the Ten Commandments. If there was something I didn't know about a tract, I'd ask my husband. He didn't know all the answers, but he always did his best to recall what he had heard things from his grandfather and grandmother from his childhood. He himself had witnessed a lot of things, so he always tried to share with me in ways that were interesting.

We confessed if we had done anything wrong. My mother-in-law had taught me how to pray for repentance, how to pray for thanksgiving, and how to pray for the meal. The material from the church had also taught me how to pray. It was very simple, clear, and detailed. What we learned from them became our way of life. We did this every Sunday. We did not know how to close the worship, so we prayed the Lord's Prayer together and sang a few hymns. One person led the singing, and the rest of the family followed.

When my mother-in-law visited us, we would pray for the meal. We prayed, "God, thank you for giving us daily bread. Thank you. Lord, please guide us not to sin." We discipled our children to pray this way. I also discipled my children to pray to God about whatever was on their minds and whatever they were seeking. My husband and I pray like that. We have spent all night praying together like that. I am not sure if it was due to our prayers or not, but our life was very stable compared to others.

Let me tell you how we tithed. No church exists in North Korea. There is no place or pastor we can offer our tithe to. But my mother-in-law emphasized the importance of tithing. So even though we did not know how to offer our tithe, we always did—by using it to help others.

When the poor could not pay for medicine or treatment, we just took care of them. We gave them medicine even if we suffered a loss. We bought rice for the hungry people, and we let them pay us back later. We gave our extra clothes to others. When we bought groceries, we did not receive any change from old ladies or mothers with children. When they weighed vegetables on the scales, we just trusted them. We did not question it.

And we considered all of this our tithe. We called it "evangelism" but couldn't even say the word aloud. When we visited our siblings, they would be happy if we brought something for them. We did not have enough, but we always prepared something for our siblings. We brought medicine or gave them a treat when we visited.

All forms of idolatry also became off-limits for us. My mother-in-law hated that Christians visited shamans and bowed to statues of dead people. She said we shouldn't do those things. So we didn't.

In the beginning, when we began to evangelize our brothers and sisters, they said, "Are you insane?" Some did go on to believe quickly, but some of them did not. Some said it was a lie. Eventually, however, they compared their lives to our life, and they started to realize that we were right. They understood that unbelief was the reason North Korea was so poor no matter how hard Kim Jong Il tried to make it prosper. Up until we left North Korea, we taught them: God exists, God is above Kim Jong Il, we should not worship Kim Jong Il, we must rely on God when we are in difficult times, we should not sin, we must give thanks to God for food and clothing, we must live for our neighbors, and so on. We could not reach out to just anyone, but we evangelized people within the framework of family.

They often joined us in our prayer for the meal. They didn't report us to authorities because they were family. And we did not let them eat food without prayer. We could not tell others, but our family came to understand that worshipping Kim Il Sung and Kim Jong Il was idolatry. We told them, "Do not have other gods in our presence. Obey God only. No one is holy but God. Do not listen to others." We evangelized them, despite not knowing how to.

Our family finally decided to defect from North Korea because of my husband. The state political security department kept monitoring him. We would have been easy to catch because we were under close watch. Religious criminals were fettered and taken to a concentration camp. And then there were our children. Since we discipled our children as Christians at home, we worried that they would make mistakes outside our home. They were very innocent. So, we decided to escape from North Korea for the future of our children.

It was very difficult to think about leaving. This was, after all, the land of our brothers and sisters and mothers and fathers and grandmothers and grandfathers. But in the matter of loyalty, the Lord had given me what my earthly parents could never give. My earthly parents had given me every ounce of love and effort they could muster, and they had never held back anything. But now I lived with a heart filled with thanks to the Lord who is always with us, always watching us, and always leading us.

As I looked up at the foreboding mountains that no feet dared traverse, where shortly my own feet and that of my children would follow the path that my husband had himself taken months earlier as he departed from the land of our birth, I treasured up in my heart a scripture, Isaiah 41:10 (NIV):

> *So do not fear, for I am with you;*
> *do not be dismayed, for I am your God.*
> *I will strengthen you and help you;*
> *I will uphold you with my righteous right hand.*

It is a gift no earthly parent can give.

5. FAMILY:

Emmanuel

From Mrs. Bae

One late November day in 2009, my daughter, my son, and I walked out our front door in North Korea and never looked back. We headed straight for the mountains (or straight up the mountains, more accurately). The reason why is because we lacked the necessary travel permit from the North Korean government that would have enabled us to pass openly through the North Korean cities along our route or to visit China legally. Everyone who desires to travel anywhere in North Korea has to have a travel document—an internal passport of sorts with an official stamp on it. It can take months to get, cost a hundred dollars or more per person, and almost certainly wouldn't have been granted to the wife and children of a man who had recently defected. So we headed for the mountains.

My husband left months before we did, to scout out the best route and prepare our way. Along our journey, in those few places where the reception and the security situation were good, he guided us as best he could through necessarily brief cell phone calls. Of course, it was difficult to pick our way through unfamiliar mountains, cities, and checkpoints by relying only on directions hastily relayed over the phone. God would have to be our Navigator.

We walked all day, every day. One day, in a city in North Korea with lax security, we were able to arrange for a car to carry us for a few hours without us having to show any permits. On another day in another village at the base of another cluster of mountains, we visited a house and told them that we were heading to a city up near the border to visit my mother-in-law and had lost our travel permits. They kindly directed us to a train station. As is typical in North Korea, we had to wait for that train for ten days, and even then we couldn't ride it very far.

These were the exceptional days, however. Most of the time, we just walked—or, rather, hiked, since 70 percent of North Korea is composed of mountains, and mountains stand as sentries over the few gaps left by North Korea's guards, police, and security agents.

Thinking back, it seems unbelievable to me that we survived. I still wonder how it all happened. The woods in the mountains we climbed were so dense and tangled that on many occasions, we couldn't even see the sky directly above us. And more times than you (or even I today) can imagine, we pushed slowly and painfully forward through frigid snowdrifts, packed chest-high. There was no other choice, no other direction to go but through.

Since my husband wasn't with us, there was no one I and my children could call out to for help when we were in trouble—except God. And I believe God walked by my side during those interminable days in as real and present a way as my children did. In the Bible, Isaiah the prophet cried out, "Emmanuel"—God with us—and so God was to us, walking with us, almost always unrecognized by us, like Christ on the road to Emmaus.

Only we walked a lot farther than Emmaus, and it was a lot more expensive. As the light would fade each day, we would head for the nearest village and stay in whatever home looked the safest, in exchange for payment. I'd ask the owner of each home for help, telling them that my mother-in-law lived up by the border and confessing that we were basically lost on the way there—which was actually quite true. In each place, God arranged for some person or family who was willing to let us spend the night in their home for about a dollar—quite a daily miracle of hospitality given how dangerous it can be to take in a stranger in North Korea.

None of the families had much money, and a dollar was enough to buy a kilogram of rice—enough to feed a family for a day. They would feed us too—sometimes more food than we thought we could eat. We North Koreans may all have been close to starving, but most of us were still clinging to our humanity, still doing our best to show care and hospitality, still seeking to carry on the customs we had learned from our youth.

And it was a good thing each family was so hospitable because we needed as much nutrition as we could get. My daughter was pregnant at the time—as is often the case with defectors, she had to leave her husband behind, else he would have had to bring his whole family too—and you'll recall that my own health was a regular struggle. And sons in North Korea are no different than sons anywhere—they always need to eat.

Each dawn would bring a good-bye to our hosts, followed by another draining day of walking and hiking and hiding. On the eighth day, we passed thirteen guard posts—they were multiplying as we moved toward the border. All we had with us were a few changes of clothes and the barest essentials, which certainly made us look suspicious. Whenever anyone asked us where we were going, we told them we were going to visit my parents-in-law near the border. Despite the number of guards we passed, they never seemed to notice us or demand our paperwork. Emmanuel.

During the day, I often stopped to ask people for directions, and somehow God always arranged for us to run into others going the same way. The biggest problem, though, was that the closer we came to the border, the more worn out we were from travel. Each time a guard post came into view, in order to avoid scrutiny we had to act like people on a very enjoyable trip to visit relatives who of course would have happily shown you their travel permits if you stopped them and asked, not like worn-out vagabonds aching from pushing uphill through chest-high snow, fatigued beyond belief from kilometer after kilometer of evading the authorities, eyes trained to the border, hearts bent on defection.

But God always sent someone to refresh us and deliver his care to us whenever we thought all was lost. Through his grace, we even got to spread his love along the way. One time we stayed with a middle-aged woman who was in terrible pain due to a stomach ailment. I had prescription medicines with me for my own difficult medical conditions, so I gave her some of my medicine. Immediately her condition began to improve. I offered to give her all my medicine and the equivalent of about three dollars if she would go with us and help us, which she was able to do for two days. Traveling without a permit and with strangers in North Korea was of course quite risky for her, so her accompaniment was really a sacrifice, especially given her illness. I gave her my sister's phone number and urged her to call if she became sick again. We may have been running for our lives, but we were still Christians running for our lives.

Our sleep in the middle-aged woman's home was sweet and deep. Thinking back on it, I can see that God's invisible hand was tenderly cradling each one of us. God knew that the woman needed medicine, so he arranged for us to show up with nowhere else to stay. My daughter, who was pregnant at the time, needed sleep, so he arranged for the middle-aged woman to cross our path. And I, maybe more than anyone, needed the rest to clear my head for the challenges ahead: The closer we came to the border, the more the spoken dialect would change and the harder—and riskier—it would be to ask anyone for help. Spies and guards abounded.

In that region, they use trucks for public transportation, not buses. Unfortunately, without a travel permit, the middle-aged woman was unable to accompany us any farther. We were on our own again, with no knowledge of the local area and our accents increasingly marking us out as strangers the farther we got away from home.

At the first checkpoint we encountered, a guard approached to inspect the truck, while we collectively held our breaths and tried to appear relaxed. Much to our surprise and relief, the guard waved us through after little more than a quick glance. But when we came to a second post—this one operated by state security personnel—they started unloading everything from the truck and examining it carefully. Our hearts raced. It must have been obvious because one of the old women in the truck sought to comfort me by whispering that if none of us had any copper, we would be okay. Copper is very valuable in China. So is tungsten. That's one reason why the North Korean government examines trucks and passengers so carefully to make sure no one is trying to smuggle these minerals out of the country. Fortunately, none of us in the truck had copper, and the guards waved us on at last.

Finally, we came to the village near the border where my mother-in-law lived. You will recall that she was the one who had led me to the Lord and who had cared for us in every possible way during her visits. She was the one who had taught us so much at our kitchen table over many nights. You may be thinking that this must have been the moment in our journey where her front door burst open and we enjoyed a warm, heartfelt reunion and many tears and prayers—or at least a warm bed and a big family dinner. But you would be forgetting where we were and what had recently happened: My husband had just defected from North Korea and was now considered an enemy of the state. His parents' home was now being watched around the clock by state security agents. The ground around the town was frozen solid. Even inside my mother-in-law's home, just about everything was frozen. And we ourselves were emotionally frozen—we who had shared so many tears and lessons and prayers could do little more than to make small talk, knowing that someone would undoubtedly be watching, listening, reporting everything.

Our encounter could only last an hour. I was sad to say good-bye, sad not to be able to enjoy deep and heartfelt conversation, sad to miss what might be her final prayers and encouragement and instruction for me this side of heaven. Still, I completely understood why we could not stay longer or say more. Now was not the time to cry or celebrate or raise any suspicions. Sometimes it is enough just to be able to look into someone else's eyes.

That is how I and my children found ourselves standing out in front of the train station trying desperately to get warm. But even standing there longer than an hour would have prompted agents to investigate, so all too soon, I had no choice but to lead my children back into the teeth of the cold as nonchalantly as I could while my mind raced, trying to figure out where we could spend the night.

I need not have worried, as God was with us and had no problem graciously providing for us yet again. We ran into a woman who was kind enough to show us somewhere we could stay. It was a man's home, and on his wall hung a special portrait of Kim Il Sung. It certainly felt a little unusual to be carrying out our defection under the eye of the Great Leader about whom I had taught so many so faithfully for so long.

It turned out that the man's wife had defected to South Korea. They didn't have problems in their relationship, he insisted; she just left to make money. But he was waiting for her to come back, longing to hear from her, not marrying anyone else. Since he lived alone and needed a way to make money, he allowed people to stay with him. He made us porridge because he had no rice, which I wasn't very happy about since I had given him money and he could have purchased some. He said that he wanted to stay in North Korea and live a good life.

My idea of the good life, however, was clearly very different than his and certainly didn't include godlike portraits of Kim Il Sung hanging on the wall. Even though the man offered to let us stay longer, we knew we needed to keep moving forward in order to avoid attracting attention.

In addition to facing the problem of an ever-decreasing number of options for lodging, we had another immediate concern: an ever-decreasing amount of money in our pockets. Though we had reached the border, we had nowhere near the money we would need to cross the river into China, nowhere near the money we would need to cross that huge country, and nowhere near the money required to cross from China into a third country to finally reach a South Korean embassy willing to receive us and transport us to South Korea. (South Korean embassies in China won't receive North Koreans for fear of the Chinese government.)

To make matters worse, the price of commodities along the border was inconceivably high. Rice, which cost two thousand North Korean won at home, here cost three hundred thousand won—more than one hundred US dollars! We exchanged what little currency we had into Chinese yuan and sewed it up into the seams of my son's clothing for safekeeping, patching over the seams in order to avoid detection.

My daughter and I started to treat those who were sick in exchange for money. We earned a little less than a dollar per patient, which not only wasn't enough to pay for our border crossing, but it wasn't even enough to pay for food or shelter to keep the three of us alive. I realized we would have to cross the river without being able to pay for any protection or assistance. It was seemingly the most desperate kind of exodus, the kind that often led to defectors being captured—or executed.

We walked along the edge of the river for several days, looking for the best place to cross. The problem was that the best places to cross—the places with the least police presence—were by definition also the most dangerous, with natural barriers acting as a police force all their own.

Finally, we selected a location to cross. The decision came with a lot of concern for me because of my daughter's pregnancy. In order to cross the river, we'd have to first lower ourselves down a cliff face about 3½ meters high. My daughter saw my worry and urged me to trust in God—an admonition that became a whole lot easier when we found a rope nearby, which I knew was God's provision. So my son jumped down. I jumped down. And my daughter hesitated not at all, scrambling down without a trace of fear and taking off running in a mad dash with the rest of us once she reached the bottom.

The river was about 150 meters wide at that point, and we had to just throw ourselves into it and swim across it as fast as we could, ignoring the piercing liquid cold and the possible impact on my daughter's pregnancy. The last voices I heard in North Korea were the shouts of people in the city crying out, "Catch them! Catch them!" Maybe God didn't exactly part the river for us, but he restrained those who sought to do us harm until we could safely reach the other side. That was exodus enough.

Who can forget that first glimpse of the land outside of North Korea? We were greeted by a blaze of Christmas lights. Christmas—I had almost forgotten! The birth of Emmanuel, God with us: *Surely God is with us.*

But there was no time to stop, stand, reflect, or even thank him for this, as guards ply both sides of the river. Still, it was impossible not to be struck by the contrast between the panoply of lights on the China side and the impenetrable blackness of the North Korean night. On the far side of the river, the citizens had no idea it was Christmas and certainly no concept of the God who is Emmanuel.

Once we fled the riverbank and gathered our bearings, we connected with a contact my husband had arranged. The contact drove us to a house where the owner gave us clean clothes and directed us to take everything out of our pockets. The reason why was that if we were apprehended with so much as a scrap of paper with North Korean writing on it, we would immediately have been exposed as defectors illegally fleeing across China. That's why we needed the new clothes as well—to look more like Chinese Koreans, not North Koreans on the run. No explanation was necessary as far as we were concerned. We were just happy to be in a warm home in China with clean, dry clothes. We had the equivalent of sixty cents in our pockets, and we gave it all to them. But they didn't know about the money we had sewn into my son's clothes.

Before we could head into the city, we had to be thoroughly investigated by the leaders who would be helping us and other North Korean defectors to cross China. They had to make sure we weren't likely to draw pursuit from the police or to raise suspicion as we traveled.

But we had a different plan: a hired police car! My husband had arranged for one to pick us up after five days. Wisely, he knew that common cars were constantly stopped and searched because they were used so frequently to transport escaping North Koreans. But police cars? No one could imagine such vehicles being used for anything other than to drag defectors back into the darkness. It had to have been the wisdom of God, and the plan worked perfectly.

Our Korean Chinese hosts told us that God would help us, despite the fact that they themselves weren't even believers. When at last the police car came for us, our hosts advised us to pretend like we were asleep when we came to the checkpoint. As it turned out, I became seriously carsick and nearly passed out, so I didn't have to pretend at all. They let us through.

In the first Chinese city we entered, we stayed with an old lady. Now that we were settled in, I could no longer contain myself. I blurted out the request that I had had on my heart ever since I had heard from my mother-in-law about the large groups of Christians who would come together to sing, pray, and worship in broad daylight—in buildings specially set apart for that purpose, no less. Could we, I asked, go to church?

There are some very large Korean Chinese churches in northeast China, with congregations numbering literally in the thousands. Such places are well known to defecting North Koreans, who are told that if they go to a building with a cross on it, they will receive help. Problem is, my host explained to me, many North Korean defectors are captured at church, since the authorities know that North Koreans head there all the time.

But to me, it was worth the risk. I had waited for so long to be with God's family in God's house. I could hardly imagine what a "church" could be like, but, as it turned out, I knew more than I thought I did. What I mean is that church looked exactly like what happens in North Korea whenever Kim Il Sung or Kim Jong Il come to town. Everyone is gathered together and offering praise, adoration, and prayer. In North Korea, however, the "god" is visible, sitting up front (or present by his portrait in the mandatory weekly self-criticism meetings).

But in church, there was no one sitting up front. And unlike my attendance at self-criticism meetings, here I felt peace, joy, comfort—and God's holiness. That night the sermon title was "At the End of the World, the Pain Will Come," which made perfect sense to me in the midst of the journey we were on. The church was so big with so many people. Lights were twinkling everywhere. People were singing from hymnals. The praising songs were so loud and powerful. I just followed what everyone did, in complete awe. It was like I had entered heaven.

The woman we stayed with was part of a Christian family. Korean Chinese people aren't supposed to help North Koreans—it's a serious crime, in fact. The Chinese government offers rewards for Korean Chinese who report North Korean defectors and aid in their capture. Flyers are posted everywhere explaining the law. But this woman made an exception for us, and it was for a lot more than one night. A broker (a guide-for-hire who helps North Korean defectors get across China and into a third country) will only start working once there are at least ten North Koreans ready to make the trip. But there were only the three of us—my daughter, my son, and me—for nineteen days. Not only did the Christian woman not complain, she and her family stayed up late at night with us showing Christian movies. One day she even took me and my daughter to church to have our hair permed. As I share this with you now, it makes me wish I could go visit that woman again. I think about her even more than I think about my own parents.

Then, on the nineteenth day of staying in this woman's home, at the direction of my husband, I and my children took a boat to another city in China where enough other North Koreans had gathered that we could now hire a broker and cross China. When we got there, the group was already departing. A woman from North Korea translated for us. They informed us they were going to search our bodies. When they directed me to take out all the money from my purse, I did. Because there wasn't much of it, I was informed I could put it back.

Every single thing was examined, including our bodies. Although the investigators would touch our bodies claiming to be searching for this or that, we just stayed silent and didn't complain. We had been warned that women should always stay together since brokers (who are rarely Christian, or, worse, Christian in name only) are famous for behaving inappropriately toward female defectors. That, of course, made me worry about my daughter. Still, the brokers were the only people we could trust at all, so all we could do was stick together and pray for them to transport us safely.

I let them have my entire suitcase, only keeping some underwear. But they found the home remedies that had been made by my daughter. God had given her the gift of healing. When my husband was doing international trade, he would pick the natural ingredients for her and she used them to make medicines. The investigators took it all: water buffalo horns, opium extract, acupuncture needles, and all our acupuncture tools. These may sound to Westerners like unusual medicine, but in North Korea, they can mean the difference between life and death. For example, one day on our journey before they took our medicines, there was a young man in a family we had made friends with. My daughter made a medicine for him because his leg was badly injured. A shaman told them that if the son were healed from this injury, his father would die early. So, his mother denied him the medicine, and the boy ended up dying.

But even these medicines weren't much use without a medical book—it had taken us three years to compile, as we learned the traditions handed on to us by others. That book was eventually taken from us too. In fact, by the time I arrived in South Korea, the only things I had left from my previous life were the watch my husband bought for me and some clothes from North Korea. Although they aren't that nice, I can still smell my hometown on them.

Unfortunately, our journey across China almost got us returned to our hometown even before we'd begun. That's because when we boarded the train, one defector girl with us started whining in North Korean that she wanted bread. The language was a dead giveaway of our identity and our flight. The eyes of the twenty-seven people in the train car turned to her. My son urged me to pray for her. When I did, she fell asleep and the compartment became quiet. But after she woke up, she began to cry again, and we were finally caught in a check. A woman hid the girl behind her and told the guard in Chinese that the girl didn't speak well yet. She gave him some money to make up for the trouble, and, mercifully, the danger passed.

We stayed in an upper berth on the train. After two days, the broker finally gave us something to eat. Perhaps he had pity on us, or perhaps he realized it would be less expensive than continuing to bribe guards if we were to complain. As for me, even when food arrived, I was unable to eat it due to that extreme motion sickness I always get. So they shifted me off the train and onto a truck with some other men. The air outside made me feel a little better. And after all the effort it took to cross North Korea on foot, crossing the enormous distance of China by truck while motion sick was still a much more bearable challenge.

Eventually, we arrived at the Mekong River, where China borders Laos. When we got there, we found a human corpse beside the river—wordless testimony to the reality that danger was still omnipresent. Those who saw the scene were filled with fear, but the experience pulled us all together. The team acted with one heart and mind helping one another, since the cost of going it alone had now been impressed upon us rather unforgettably.

A boat arrived and our family had to be divided because our part of the group had arrived last of all. My son and I were herded onto one boat while my daughter was herded onto another. We prayed fervently that God would keep her safe and help us navigate the river safely all the way to Thailand, where we would then make for the South Korean embassy.

After six hours on the river, we stopped to rest, eat, and change from Chinese boats to Laotian ones. Eventually, we arrived at our destination, a port in Thailand. I found myself chosen as the de facto leader of twenty-seven defectors, tasked with making sure that we all stayed together. Because we didn't know where we could find the embassy, we decided to go to the police and turn ourselves in. Though, in China, we would have been sent back to North Korea, here in Thailand, we knew that we would be held in prison but then sent on to South Korean custody.

In jail, we met our first South Koreans, representatives of the government who were sent to greet us. At that time,

I had a cross-shaped brooch that I had kept hidden while in North Korea that I rejoiced at being able to wear openly now. The South Korean translator, a Christian, saw it and greeted me joyfully. While many North Koreans come to meet Christ along the defection route, my brooch signaled that I had been a Christian from even before my defection. We would later discover how rare that was, learning from many South Koreans that we were the only North Koreans they had ever heard of who had been practicing Christians inside North Korea before visiting China. That is because most practicing Christians in North Korea end up in concentration camps or prisons like my husband had. I was reminded again that only God—who must have had a purpose for our defection—could have made our journey successful.

We stayed in the Thai jail that night, as is customary for all North Korean defectors. The South Korean government needs to weed out North Korean spies, not to mention Korean Chinese people pretending to be North Korean in an effort to resettle in South Korea. So the investigation process is quite intensive and, I would discover, quite expensive as well. I thought we would only be in jail for the night. But when we went to court, a Thai policeman came close to me to show me a document and said, "You were illegally staying in Thailand. Pay the penalty." So we prepared about a hundred dollars each. Unfortunately, we couldn't understand how and when and to whom to pay this "penalty," so we ended up staying in the jail for another five days, which cost another two dollars per person per day. Still, we didn't complain. The jail had good blankets and nice floors, and we were able to take showers with clean water. As for the food, we didn't like the smell much, so we would wait to eat until the evening when we could put red pepper paste all over it without insulting anyone. My son even put on weight because we were eating so well. North Koreans would be willing to live in that jail permanently if you asked them to.

Not all the difficulties were behind us, however. We were transported to a second prison, which was much more like a real prison. Apparently, a lot of North Koreans starved to death there for lack of money and help. Caring defectors who had come before us had scrawled messages on the wall to let us know how to stay alive and make it through the place—who to pay, how much, where to go, and where not to. The greatest thrill came when my son found a message my husband had etched there in an effort to be helpful to those who would follow him—maybe for us specifically. It read, "Money is needed to come to the next prison[.] It takes 650 won for bus fare. If you can't pay it, you'll starve to death."

Since we had the money, we only had to stay for one day before being sent to Bangkok. If all this sounds like a disorganized whirlwind, it's because it was—and still is, for every North Korean defector who makes the journey. One minute they would herd us into a restaurant in Bangkok and serve us a pretty decent meal, and the next minute, they would herd us to a North Korean defector "camp" where life was horrible. Then we were sent to a holding facility for all kinds of foreigners—beggars and old people who didn't have anything but who gradually floated down the Mekong Delta to Bangkok looking for something. The place was incomprehensibly crowded, and we had no idea how long we would be there. Hours? Days?

When you are a defector, no one has to tell you anything. You just go where they make you go, stand where they make you stand, ignore it while they search you again and again, and pray for Emmanuel to remain with you and keep your family together. And you pray literally standing on one foot because the cell is too crowded for you to have both feet on the ground. Eventually, I gave in and paid two dollars to gain access to a special reserved area where we could finally sit.

Finally, after about three hours, a person from the South Korean embassy came and took us to the place where only

North Korean defectors can stay. They sat us in rows. The South Korean leader there had a haughty attitude. He directed me to write a résumé, which I did. Being that my daughter was pregnant, I helped her to get comfortable so she could relax, but I had to be a bit rude to others so we could take up more space. A mother is a mother even in prison, you know.

I rejoiced to find that there were other Christians there. They were having a worship service, so we joined them. They seemed to recognize that I had been a Christian for some time, so they asked me to lead the service. I declined and just participated. Day after day, it was how we made use of the time. Who had more to be thankful for than us? And who had more on our minds—namely, those we had left behind, and those we would see again ahead—than us?

After twenty days, they boarded us onto a plane. It was none too soon: In Thailand, defectors quickly learn that it is important to be one of the first ones to leave. We were probably given that opportunity because my daughter was pregnant. At one point during our stay, someone poked another pregnant woman's belly, killing the baby. Apparently, this person wanted to be one of the first to leave too.

We were warned not to lie and not to take a cell phone. So we did as we were told, taking our seats on the plane and craning our necks to look out the window of this flight that would, after our journey of several thousand miles, take us to a new world just a short distance away from where we had walked out our front door not many months before.

Arriving in South Korea was a different kind of disorienting than arriving in China. The language isn't identical—there's about a 40 percent divergence between North and South Korean dialects—but South Korean is still more understandable than Chinese. And Korean food is Korean food whether it's north or south of the DMZ. The biggest difference between North and South Korea is the number of cars and the much greater cleanliness of the cities. I had heard that life in South Korea was much better than our life, and now I could see it with my own eyes. Seeing all the traffic for the first time, I thought there must be a big conference everyone was going to. I soon found out that people in South Korea can go wherever they want, whenever they want—a stark contrast to our need to head for the hills because we lacked the travel permit mandated by the North Korean government.

When we arrived at the airport, we had a very good first impression of South Korea thanks to the lack of required paperwork and permits. While those who were coming from China for a trip had to get an ID card, we were citizens: All North Koreans are by definition South Korean citizens, since the Korean War never formally ended. So we didn't need any permit or permission or paperwork or anything. We are one family. Only the other North and South Koreans understand that. That made me happy. Even now, I'm thankful for that. I was as grateful at that moment in customs as I was when I first saw the Christmas lights in China.

There are a lot of things that might surprise you or puzzle you about how North Korean defectors are introduced to life in South Korea. Men and women are kept in separate facilities, for example, and not permitted to communicate—not even husbands and wives or parents and children. Such precautions are related to the growing number of spies posing as defectors, sent by the North Korean government to infiltrate South Korean society. Just as in North Korea, whenever three people are gathered together, one of them is likely to be a spy. Life for North Koreans entering South Korea isn't much different—spies are everywhere. So examinations and investigations form the daily routine for defectors for months. We were examined, investigated, and also oriented to life in South Korea, first for three months in one South Korean government facility and then for another three months in another. My daughter was permitted to leave earlier due to her pregnancy.

As for me, there were church services there in the naturalization facilities, and I had a lot to learn and a long journey from which to recover. There are North Koreans who live illegally in China for several years before making the grueling trip to South Korea, and those defectors often marry several times, have many children here and there, sometimes do things they want to hide, and can't avoid having a lot of flaws of the kind that interest government investigators. By comparison, we were delightfully dull. The South Korean staff treated us well because we were only in China for a few weeks. Still, I couldn't meet my son or my husband there, since they were being similarly investigated in the corresponding facility for men. So I wondered what it would be like to see my husband again after so long. It turned out it was almost identical to when I met him the first time, at the North Korean college many years before.

You'll recall at that time how we passed each other with only the fewest of words exchanged between us. Now, at the end of February 2010, I ran into my husband while we were all on a field trip eating a meal at a South Korean restaurant. We weren't permitted even to say hello to each other at that time, but we did get to greet each other with a nod. And this meeting was a little more romantic than the first encounter we ever had: When I was going upstairs, he made a little heart sign with his hands to say that he loved me. And I did the same in reply.

Gradually, we all completed our time at the naturalization facility and were released one by one. When my husband got out, my daughter was waiting for him with her brand-new baby on her back. As soon as my husband saw our daughter, he didn't hug her like in a TV drama, but they tapped each other on the shoulder and came home together by bus. Some taps and bus rides are better and deeper than hugs or TV shows.

When I got out of government resettlement center with my son, we went to my daughter's place. The trip there was painful because I got carsick again. But when we arrived there, I still remember the scene: my husband, daughter and granddaughter looking down at us through the window. *These are the generations...*

In sheer joy, my husband ran downstairs to greet us. You may wonder what warm and romantic thing he said to me at that moment, but actually what he did was to explain to us how to use the elevator. After all, we were not quite done with our journey yet—we were all standing in the lobby, overwhelmed by emotion—and he intended to care for us every last step of the way just as he had since the beginning, even to our daughter's living room. I cannot even express how happy I was at that moment. Even though I had been able to see my daughter and grandchild when they visited me at the naturalization facility, I couldn't help but cry when I saw them again. I think we must cry when we feel extremely happy to meet somebody.

We kept patting one another, talking through the night. It had, after all, been a year since we had all been together. My son was now a year taller—and fatter too!—and my daughter had given birth to a baby. We learned how my husband made his way to South Korea, and all that he had done to prepare our way too. I couldn't help but burst into tears as I tried to take it all in. We just kept talking until 5:00 a.m., and even then we couldn't sleep. We filled the refrigerator with meat, fish, and fruits. My husband was so happy, saying, "The TV works well, and we have working water! Keep washing!"

A whole book could be written just about our time in South Korea so far—all the discoveries and reunions and wonderful moments we've had in church and in grocery stores and in speaking to people across South Korea and even around the world about our time in North Korea. But that's not the book the Lord directed us to write.

The book the Lord directed us to write began with a grandfather stretching his arms out across the doorway of a church building in China nearly a century ago. And now it is time for that book to end in the same way it began, because these are the generations of the Bae family, and the testimony given to us to receive and pass on to you is the story of Emmanuel, the God of our exodus. And your exodus too.

On January 9, 2011, at 1:00 a.m., my parents-in-law were due to be picked up by a car we had arranged for them to take across the border into China, where they would then be escorted all the way to South Korea. Now in their eighties, we wanted the trip to be as easy for them as possible.

At 5:00 a.m., we still had not heard from the broker who was supposed to meet them on the China side of the border. We called him on the phone. No news, he said. They had not yet arrived

They would, it turned out, never arrive.

After several days, my husband called friends of my parents-in-law. "Your parents were caught. If you keep calling me, they'll arrest me too. Don't call me," came the urgent whisper on the other end of the phone line.

In July of 2011, we learned that my parents-in-law had been taken to a concentration camp. Evangelism in North Korea will always land you there, sooner or later.

And I suspect, the more that I get to know the world outside of North Korea, that boldly living for the Gospel will get you in trouble pretty much anywhere you live. "In fact," the apostle Paul tells young Timothy in 2 Timothy 3:12 (NIV), "everyone who wants to live a godly life in Christ Jesus will be persecuted."

Concentration camps in North Korea are places of unimaginable darkness. Almost no one ever escapes from a concentration camp, and certainly no one is ever released. Instead, each prisoner is given a miniscule ration of gruel, carefully calculated to keep the prisoner alive long enough until another prisoner is brought in to take his or her place.

This is where my parents-in-law were sent. This is where they are now living out the end of their days. In their eighties, they are nameless, faceless cogs in the largest network of concentration camps ever operated in human history. Every day for them must be a backbreaking nightmare.

So perhaps you are sad or disappointed that the book we were commanded by God to write is now ending. If so, let me share with you something that I hope may encourage you: *this may be where the book ends, but the story of the generations will continue until Emmanuel returns.*

When my husband was little, my husband's mother asked my husband's grandfather, "Dad, did you really hear God's voice?" When he told her yes, she pressed him for all the details. He shared how God's voice had been especially clear to him when he had been fasting, praying, or sleeping. My mother-in-law told him that she'd like to hear God as he had heard. She was sad that she couldn't hear God, and she prayed for a faith as deep as his.

When my husband was a boy, he and his family were exiled to the barren countryside when his mother refused to turn away even a criminal in need. And when her husband reminded her that it was this kindness that had consigned the family to such a place, she replied, "We should always live out our faith every moment and never let it be shaken."

When things worsened, she asked her family matter-of-factly, "Why am I supposed to be afraid of anything? God is on my side, and he'll make a way for us. Even in the hard times, he'll solve all our problems. Why should we focus on the difficulties?"

Somewhere in a concentration camp in North Korea today, a prisoner is hearing for the first time about Noah's Ark, Sodom and Gomorrah, and the way people were created, all because God loves people so much that he will even send his short, stoop-shouldered eighty-year-old messenger into a concentration camp to tell them the good news.

*The light shines in the darkness, and the darkness has not—*cannot—*overcome it* (John 1:5, NIV).

The generations continue, and always will. And my mother-in-law's best ministry and deepest faith, as well as my own—and yours too—are yet ahead.

AFTERWORD:
From the Rev. Eric Foley

A little over a hundred years ago, Pyongyang—which is today the capital of North Korea—was the site of a revival so large that the city came to be known as the "Jerusalem of the East."[xix] The revival occurred in January 1907 during a prayer meeting at what was then the largest church in Korea, the First Church of Pyongyang. William Blair, a missionary who was at that prayer meeting, called it "The Korean Pentecost." He said, "The prayer sounded to me like the falling of many waters, an ocean of prayer beating against God's throne."[xx]

That story about the Great Pyongyang Revival of 1907 is well known. There is, however, a more obscure story that occurred on the second day of the revival. As everyone at the church was rejoicing over this miraculous outpouring, God sent a powerful sign of what was to come.

> [Pastor] Choo... one of the first Korean leaders to graduate from Presbyterian College and Theological Seminary and later the pastor of First Church of Pyongyang, was asked to preach [on the second day of the revival]... He literally *"had himself all tied up and was struggling to get out.* He said, *'This is what revival does. It tears away your sins and sets you free."* [xxi]

113

The revival had come, and people were ecstatic. They shouted, "This is true freedom!" But through Pastor Choo, God wanted to give the church a new understanding of freedom: not freedom the way the world gives it or understands it, but freedom in Christ, which usually looks like bondage to the world. During his sermon, Pastor Choo did not burst out of his bonds. Instead, he proclaimed faithfully from within them—the way the North Korean church has done for the more than one hundred years of its existence.

Kim Il Sung led a systematic extermination of Christians through the first twenty years of his regime. He was so successful that to this day historians have scant evidence that Christians even existed in North Korea from the late 1960s to the early 1990s. The story of the Baes is historical verification of what we learn theologically from 1 Kings 19:18: God always preserves a remnant that neither kneels to false gods nor kisses them.

North Korea may be the first nation on earth where the church has been reseeded largely by martyrs. The one hundred thousand believers currently in North Korea were raised up surrounded by the blood of many faithful witnesses—as were many other North Koreans who put their faith in Christ and have already been put to death for their confession.

An estimated thirty thousand of today's North Korean Christians—Mr. Bae's mother and father among them—are living out their faith in concentration camps. Our first instinct is to work tirelessly to free them. But our second instinct ought to be to remember that God does not look at freedom the same way we do. An estimated one hundred fifty thousand to two hundred thousand North Koreans are prisoners in those camps.[xxii] Many will end their days there. How could a God of boundless love not reach out personally to comfort those people, assuring them that they are not forgotten? And, if he did reach out, why wouldn't he do it the way he always has—through people he has specially trained for the task, in barren fields and temporary exiles, whom he has walked with daily and who he speaks to as his friends?

"Remember those who are in prison," we are admonished in Hebrews 13:3 (ESV), "as though in prison with them." If we are not careful, we will misread this verse as a call to pity Christians like Mr. Bae's parents. But if we are careful, we will read it as a call to imitate them. This does not mean that we will march to the concentration camp door, knock on it, and demand to be admitted any more than it did for the Baes or the first Christians. Instead, it means that when we find ourselves in dark places, rather than focusing our thoughts on escape, we will instead seek to emit light. Or, as Mr. Bae's mother once said, "Why am I supposed to be afraid of anything? God is on my side, and he'll make a way for us. Even in the hard times, he'll solve all our problems. But why should we focus on the difficulties?"

It is the same message the resurrected Jesus shared with the apostle Peter as they walked together along the seashore. "When you were younger you dressed yourself and went where you wanted," Jesus said in John 21:18 (NIV), "but when you are old you will stretch out your hands, and someone else will dress you and lead you where you do not want to go." And, we might fairly add, when you find yourself there, emit light.

The Lord granted Mr. Bae's mother's prayer for faith as deep as her father's. There are few well-lit and comfortable paths to such a place. May the Almighty God of the Baes bless them with continued faithful service across all their generations until he returns. And may we imitate them as they continue to imitate him, even in the darkest place in the darkest country on earth.

See a video interview with Mr. Bae and learn more about North Korean Christians!

Seoul USA is a registered nonprofit organization in both America and South Korea. Our mission is to serve as a convening mechanism for ordinary Christians in North and South Korea, Asia, and the West to grow to fullness in Christ through hearing and doing the Word together.

Visit www.seoulusa.org for the largest collection of free resources and information about the North Korean Underground Church, including a video interview with Mr. Bae.

For up-to-the-minute updates on North Korean Christians, connect with us on Facebook at www.facebook.com/seoulusa.

For in-depth Christian analysis and commentary on the situation in North Korea, see Pastor Foley's weekly blog posts at www.ericfoley.com.

Seoul USA
14960 Woodcarver Road
Colorado Springs, CO 80923
719-481-4408

The Voice of the Martyrs is a Christian organization that serves persecuted Christians around the world. The ministry helps Christians living in nations hostile to the gospel, including Communist and Islamic countries. Founded in 1967 by Richard and Sabina Wurmbrand, a Romanian couple once imprisoned for their faith, The Voice of the Martyrs has a network of offices around the globe dedicated to helping persecuted Christians. The ministry fulfills the Wurmbrands' vision of raising awareness about the plight of the persecuted and assisting those suffering for their Christian witness. VOM accomplishes this through five main purposes:

1. To encourage and empower Christians to fulfill the Great Commission in areas of the world where they are persecuted for sharing the gospel of Jesus Christ.

2. To provide practical relief and spiritual support to the families of Christian martyrs.

3. To equip persecuted Christians to love and win to Christ those who are opposed to the gospel in their part of the world.

4. To undertake projects of encouragement, helping believers rebuild their lives and Christian witness in countries where they have formerly suffered oppression.

5. To promote the fellowship of all believers by informing the world of the faith and courage of persecuted Christians, thereby inspiring believers to a deeper level of commitment to Christ and involvement in His Great Commission.

VOM publishes a free newsletter that shares the courageous stories of our persecuted family worldwide and ways you can help.

For more information, contact VOM at:

PO Box 443
Bartlesville, OK 74005-0443
tel: 800-747-0085
e-mail: thevoice@vom-usa.org
Website: www.persecution.com

ENDNOTES:

i International Institute for Strategic Studies; Hackett, James (ed.) (3 February 2010). The Military Balance 2010. London: Routledge, 411-413.

ii Defence Forum India, "New Threat from N.Korea's 'Asymmetrical' Warfare," April 29, 2010, http://defenceforumindia.com/showthread.php?t=9887&page=1.

iii Offshore-Advisors.com, "The Underground Economy," January 8, 2011, http://www.offshore- advisors.com/the-underground-economy.html.

iv Bill Powell and Adam Zagorin, "The Tony Soprano of North Korea," Time, July 12, 2007, http://www.time.com/time/magazine/article/0,9171,1642898,00.html.

v Adherents.com, "Discussion of Why Juche Is Classified as a Major World Religion," April 23, 2005, http://www.adherents.com/largecom/Juche.html.

vi Andrei Lankov, North of the DMZ: Essays on Daily Life in North Korea (Jefferson, NC: McFarland & Company, 2007), 33-37. See also Kondgan Oh, "North Korea: The Nadir of Freedom," Foreign Policy Research Institute, May 2007, http://www.fpri.org/footnotes/1216.200705.oh.northkorea.html.

vii World Center for North Korea Missions, "A Look at Christianity in North Korea," April 15, 2002, http://www.crosswalk.com/1135128/.

viiiThe Voice of the Martyrs, "This Is Our Victory," October 2008, http://www.persecution.com/uploads/media/downloads/117_ThisisOurVictory-October2008.pdf.

ix SatBytes, "Did North Korea Launch a Satellite?," 2006, http://www.spacetoday.org/Satellites/SatBytes/NoKoreaSat.html.

x NorthKoreaChristians.com, "North Korea Religion," 2009,http://www.northkoreanchristians.com/religion- north-korea.html.

xi NorthKoreanChristians.com, "North Korea Religion," 2009, http://www.northkoreanchristians.com/religion- north-korea.html.

xii Michael Bristow, "North Korea: Life in Cultural Isolation," BBC News Magazine, December 20, 2011, http://www.bbc.co.uk/news/magazine-16243995. See also Sunny Lee, "God Forbid, Religion in North Korea?," Asia Times Online, May 12,

2007, http://www.atimes.com/atimes/Korea/IE12Dg01.html.

xiii Anne Penketh, "God Is Dead. Long Live Kim Il Sung," The Independent (UK), September 17, 2004, http://www.rickross.com/reference/nkorea/nkorea27.html.

xiv Information from here through the end of the chapter comes from Seoul USA, "The History of the North Korean Underground Church," 2012, http://www.seoulusa.org/mediafiles/2012-03-susa-k-newsletter.pdf.

xv Park Hyun Min, "Believers at Pyongyang Bongsu Church are Members of Chosun Workers Party," Daily NK, June 8, 2007, http://www.dailynk.com/english/read.php?cataId=nk01600&num=2194.

xvi Chosunilbo, "More N.Korean Workers to Earn Valuta for Kim Jong-un," english.chosun.com, April 27, 2012, http://english.chosun.com/site/data/html_dir/2012/04/27/2012042701255.html.

xvii Paula Hancocks, "North Korean defector stands for South Korean election," CNN U.S., April 10, 2012, http://articles.cnn.com/2012-04-10/asia/world_asia_north-korea-defector_1_cho-north-korea- defectors?_s=PM:ASIA.

xviii See 1 Kings 19:18.

xix George Thomas, "The Pyongyang Revival 100 Years Later," CBN.com, June 29, 2007, http://www.cbn.com/CBNnews/188123.aspx.

xx C. Hope Flinchbaugh, "A Century After North Korean Revival, Dreams of an Encore," Christianity Today, January 31, 2007, http://www.christianitytoday.com/ct/2007/januaryweb-only/105-32.0.html.

xxi Flinchbaugh, "A Century After North Korean Revival."

xxii Blaine Harden, Escape from Camp 14: One Man's Remarkable Odyssey from North Korea to Freedom in the West (New York: Viking, 2012), 4.